THE
GAME
OF
SOCCER

•

TED SMITS

Prentice-Hall, Inc., Englewood Cliffs, N.J.

The Game of Soccer

by Ted Smits

© 1968 by Ted Smits

Library of Congress Catalog Card Number: 68-26052

Printed in the United States of America • T

Prentice-Hall International, Inc., *London*
Prentice-Hall of Australia, Pty. Ltd., *Sydney*
Prentice-Hall of Canada, Ltd., *Toronto*
Prentice-Hall of India Private Ltd., *New Delhi*
Prentice-Hall of Japan, Inc., *Tokyo*

*Photographs by permission of the United Soccer
Association, the National Professional Soccer League,
and the North American Soccer League.*

Acknowledgment is hereby made for brief quotations
of material from *Soccer From the Press Box* by Archie
Ledbrooke & Edgar Turner. Copyright 1955 by Nicholas
Kaye Ltd by permission of Kaye & Ward Ltd.

FOR

RICHARD

AND HIS JUNIOR VARSITY SIDE

AT THE

ALLEN-STEVENSON SCHOOL

PREFACE

Soccer is the universal, world-accepted sport. Europeans and others on every continent have become so familiar with it that all literature on this grandest of games tends to become technical and involved, or else concerns itself with epochal matches or vivid personalities.

Until now, no one in North America has attempted to draw all the threads together in a single volume that will interest both those who know nothing about the game and, to a considerable extent, those who know a great deal. Here in *The Game of Soccer* is the story of the sport from the very beginning along with the strange and fascinating story of how professional soccer finally found a foothold in the United States and Canada.

The rules are described simply, hints are given on how to enjoy the game, a few of the great personalities—and great games—are sketched, and even such mysterious matters as the pool betting system are explored.

Those of us deeply concerned with the North American Soccer League are convinced that in the years ahead this great international game will establish itself as firmly in the United States and Canada as it has in every other nation of the globe —in most of which it is without challenge the national pastime. *The Game of Soccer* should make an important contribution to an understanding of the sport.

John W. Anderson II
President, Detroit Cougars and
Chairman, Executive Committee of the
North American Soccer League

CONTENTS

●

● THE GAME OF SOCCER ●

1

The birth of big-time soccer in North
America with the creation of the
United Soccer Association

————◆————

Said Ken Macker, president of the Western Conference of
the North American Soccer League, to Pete Rozelle, commissioner of professional football:

"You've stolen the name of our game. You play handball. We
play football."

Said Rozelle to Macker:

"You're stealing our crowd. You are drawing the well-dressed
and the affluent."

Said Dick Walsh, president of the Eastern Conference of the
North American Soccer League, when he saw his first game in
1957:

"My God. They have plays."

Soccer, as it is called in the United States and Canada, or
football, as it is called everywhere else in the world, has
finally come to the North American continent on a major scale.

It is a game played with the feet and a ball, the two being

1

in almost constant contact except for those moments when the skull is used as a kind of tennis racket. This is in sharp contrast to American-type football, where the foot and the ball may come together violently no more than a dozen times in a game and the hands are used constantly. Use of the hands in soccer is illegal except for the goalkeeper.

As for the plays, although the game is fluid and easy to understand, they exist in elaborate patterns, out in the open, characterized by the highest degree of skill.

| As for the crowds, while perhaps not as good for professional soccer's much-ballyhooed opening 1967 season as some had hoped, they were far from puny. The National Professional Soccer League drew a total of 818,847, and the United Soccer Association, playing an abbreviated schedule, 568,118. |

From the start soccer has been headed by two men comparable—in both stature and salary—to Pete Rozelle and General William D. Eckert, commissioners of football and baseball, respectively. The first commissioner of the National Professional Soccer League was Ken Macker; Richard Walsh was top man in the United Soccer Association. When the leagues merged, Macker became president of the Western Conference and Walsh of the Eastern Conference. Before coming to soccer Macker was a newspaper publisher and owner of a TV-radio network in the Philippines. Walsh was formerly vice-president of the Los Angeles baseball Dodgers. Oddly enough, Macker and Rozelle were once partners in P. K. Macker and Co., a successful public relations concern in San Francisco.

The arrival in the limelight of the League and the Association did not mean that soccer was making its first appearance in the United States and Canada. It had existed on the continent in various forms since the mid-1800's. Originally it was strongest on the Atlantic seaboard, particularly in New England. In 1886 international matches were played between the United States and Canada, resulting in two tie games and two victories for each team.

2

By 1900 soccer had spread across the United States, taking an unusually strong grip in St. Louis, and in 1914 the United States Football Association was formed to preside over both the professional and amateur aspects of the game. It was recognized by the Federation Internationale de Football Associations, the ruling body of world soccer, a fact that was to become of prime and expensive importance in 1967. In 1945 the word "soccer" was inserted in the Association's name to avoid public confusion. A parallel organization, the Dominion of Canada Football Association, was set up north of the border and also recognized by FIFA, pronounced "fee-fah." By the 1960's in Canada and the United States there were in excess of 3,500 soccer teams with 75,000 players, mostly amateur, and including squads in the biggest and best universities and the most exclusive public schools, as well as scores of teams supported and manned by recent immigrants and their children.

In 1960, Bill Cox, a tall and distinguished-looking sports promoter and product of Yale, took a look at the sports void in New York created by the transfer of the Brooklyn Dodgers and the New York Giants to greener baseball pastures on the Pacific Coast, and decided the time had come for the introduction of topflight professional soccer in the United States, and in New York City specifically. He once owned the Philadelphia Phillies of the National Baseball League until he tangled with Commissioner Kenesaw Mountain Landis, and later presided over the short-lived Brooklyn Dodger professional football team.

Cox founded the International Soccer League with the approval of the United States Soccer Football Association and FIFA. He brought over well-recognized European and South American teams for a summer schedule that included two games weekly in New York's Polo Grounds and one weekly in Jersey City's Roosevelt Stadium. The first year Bangu of Brazil won the 1960 league championship by defeating Kilmarnock of Scotland 2–0 before 25,440. The next year the Dukla soccer club

3

of Czechoslovakia made a sweep of the American Cup final series by downing Everton of England 2–0 before 18,737.

In 1963 the International Soccer League had to move to Randall's Island, not the most accessible of New York City stadiums, because the New York baseball Mets preempted the Polo Grounds while waiting for Shea Stadium to be built. Even there attendance continued good. Dukla won the American Cup finals again, this time defeating America of Brazil 2–1 before 20,185. In 1963 Dukla won the cup for a third time, defeating West Ham United of England. The final game before 15,231 in the Randall's Island stadium was a 1–1 tie but Dukla was awarded the cup by virtue of a previous 1–0 victory over West Ham in Chicago. In 1964 the league passed the 1,000,000-mark in attendance.

By 1965, however, differences between Cox and soccer's American ruling body, the United States Soccer Football Association, had become so profound that the International League was shelved. Cox was required to pay five percent of the gate receipts to the Association and in four years this exceeded $150,000, but relations between the promoter and the Association were always strained. International League teams had played in Chicago, Newark, Boston, Los Angeles and Chicopee, Massachusetts—an ethnic center of the sport—in addition to New York.

Then why did soccer blossom professionally and in affluence in 1967?

Spontaneous combustion is the only answer. It was not created by television as part of a sports battle between networks. The television contracts came long after the two rival leagues had been created.

To the casual observer the explanation of the rise of soccer in North America might read something like this: "The televising of the World Cup finals from London live by satellite July 30, 1966, and the thrilling game in which England defeated West Germany 4–2 in two overtimes created vast interest

4

in the United States and Canada. Then soon after on Labor Day in New York's Yankee Stadium 41,598 turned out to see Edson Arantes de Nascimento, known around the world as Pelé, lead his team, Santos of Brazil, to a 4–1 victory over Inter of Milan. So the promoters saw their chance and moved in."

But strange to say, soccer was already launched professionally, backed by millions of dollars, before either of these spectacular events. They gave a tremendous boost to the hopes of soccer's backers, but they were unrelated to its organization.

But why soccer suddenly on a big scale now?

Perhaps the promoters saw soccer as the next big audience sport on the North American horizon. After all, it is far and away the most popular sport around the world.

Perhaps they felt that the new stadiums that had mushroomed in Houston, Los Angeles and Anaheim, San Francisco, Oakland, Minneapolis-St. Paul, New York, San Diego, Milwaukee and St. Louis—with still others planned—needed something more than baseball and professional football to remain happily profitable.

Perhaps they saw in Bill Cox's International Soccer League the foundation on which big-time soccer could be built.

They decided wisely that they did not want to compete against college and professional football, which are played at the time of soccer's traditional fall and winter season elsewhere in the world.

But they felt they could compete against baseball, possibly because soccer is so different from it in philosophy, tactics, and speed, and also because except for a few instances soccer games could be scheduled when baseball teams were on the road.

In May 1966 Bill Cox, feeling that the time was ripe for a broad-based professional soccer league in the United States and Canada, asked forty men with sports backgrounds and substantial bank accounts to meet at the Yale Club in New York. Cox, a persuasive man, outlined budgets and described the apparatus of recruiting soccer players.

5

There was manifest enthusiasm. There were also individual conflicts. Some promoters wanted cities that already had been spoken for. A splinter group developed that included John Pinto of RKO-General, a corporation with widely diversified interests. Bob Hermann, a wealthy St. Louis sportsman, remained with Cox. To replace those lost, John W. Allyn of the Chicago baseball White Sox and Jack Kent Cooke, the millionaire ex-Canadian promoter who was establishing roots in Los Angeles, were invited in. Ex-Senator Fred Keating was proposed as commissioner.

The splinter group, and a very hefty splinter it was, included in addition to Pinto, Dan Rooney of the Pittsburgh football Steelers, and James Millen, a Los Angeles attorney.

Then came another fracture. Cooke and Allyn, both strong-willed men, left the Cox–Hermann league.

So by mid-1966 there were three soccer leagues in the process of gestation. Now came the all-important maneuvering for recognition by the United States Soccer Football Association, which would carry with it the sanction of FIFA and status in soccer the world around.

All this sudden and substantial promotional interest came as a pleasant surprise to the Association. This comparatively obscure governing body of a minor American sport housed in a tiny office in midtown New York held a most precious power. It ruled soccer, amateur and professional, in the United States. It did so by virtue of being the sole United States representative of FIFA, which in turn governs world soccer with an iron hand. The United States Soccer Football Association, furthermore, was recognized by the United States Olympic Committee and the Amateur Athletic Union.

This is the way all worldwide sports operate. There is a central, international governing body for every sport, and in each nation there is a separate national organization with close ties to the international group. When a league or club wins the approval of the national group this automatically carries

6

with it the blessing of the international body. Thus the International Amateur Athletic Federation, world governing body of track and field, recognizes in the United States only the Amateur Athletic Union, and from this has developed the long, complex, exasperating struggle between the AAU and the National Collegiate Athletic Association. Professional baseball, not yet widespread enough to justify an international organization, generally looks to the American commissioner as the ruling head all the way from the Caribbean to Japan.

At its 1965 national meeting, the United States Soccer Football Association had dreamed of one national professional soccer league and even set up a committee to explore its possibilities. But no one imagined there would be the interest that subsequently developed.

James P. McGuire, FIFA's representative in the United States and a power in the United States Soccer Football Association, was alarmed at the rivalries that had developed. He held more than a score of meetings with the three factions in an effort to achieve a merger. What he wanted was the best of all three groups but he failed. The Association decided to test the financial determination of the three rivals. It asked for a bond of $5,000 and then boosted this to $50,000. Two of the groups put up the money but the Cox–Hermann league did not because of Cox's deeply felt suspicion of the Association.

Gene Edwards, who headed the Association subcommittee assigned the job of exploring the development of professional soccer, admitted, "You can imagine the committee's surprise when not one but three separate bids were tendered to do the job. The feeling of the sub-committee must have been one of mixed emotions, something akin to watching one's mother-in-law drive your new Cadillac convertible off a cliff . . .

"Three separate plans were submitted. Each was somewhat different in structure, yet somewhat overlapping in design, modus operandi and personnel. For the purpose of this report

7

I will refer to them in the following order and not in their importance, chronologically.

"One, a group headed by Mr. Richard Millen of Los Angeles.

"Two, a group headed by Mr. Robert Hermann of St. Louis.

"Three, a group headed by Mr. Jack Kent Cooke of Los Angeles."

Edwards concluded his 1966 report to the United States Soccer Football Association by recommending approval of Cooke's league and the motion was carried almost unanimously. Later it became known that the international governing body of soccer, FIFA, anxious to launch the game massively in the one prosperous and civilized part of the world where it had not yet taken solid root, had urged the Association to recognize only individual teams rather than an entire league. Had this advice been followed, and a single team picked in each major city, much costly infighting could have been avoided. However in 1966 the clear feeling of the Association was that in recognizing Cooke's league, the other two groups were disposed with once and for all. With Cooke's organization the only one left in the field, everything was to proceed in an orderly manner. Cooke expansively told the convention after he had been anointed:

"Not one of you is going to be disappointed. . . . We are dedicated to one job only—to make a shining success out of soccer. It is not just with the money, as I said before; we are going to condition our public and condition our agents to this great game of soccer. Then, in the late spring of 1968, we are going to introduce this game as the coming game in America and it is going to be a very real and firm and shining success for all of you and all of us here."

The Association's contract with Cooke and his league was an exclusive one and according to the international rules no other soccer teams dared poach on their domain in Canada and the United States. For the United States Soccer Football Association, which for years had led a hand-to-mouth existence, it would be highly lucrative. Each of the twelve teams was to pay the Association the flat sum of $25,000 to be used for the development of soccer generally, plus four percent of all gate receipts. In addition, ten percent of the devoutly-to-be-hoped-for television revenues would go into the Association's coffers.

In return the Association, and of course FIFA, recognized the new league as the sole authentic, respectable, true-blue soccer organization in the United States and Canada. After careful planning extending through 1967, play would formally start in 1968. The new organization was christened as the North American Soccer League. This was subsequently changed to United Soccer Association whose initials, USA, have a pleasantly patriotic ring.

The future of soccer seemed rosy.

2

The emergence of a rival league, the
National Professional Soccer League,
in defiance of the soccer Establishment

———◆———

The United States Soccer Football Association failed to reckon with the promoters who had been left out in the cold. The two disappointed leagues met in Chicago in the autumn of 1966 and, burying old enmities, formed the National Professional Soccer League, admittedly without national or international approval. It was in fact during the first year of its existence an outlaw league. To get New York into the National League, John Pinto and RKO-General bought out the franchise held by Bill Cox. The price was fixed by arbitration. Cox took a franchise for Hartford, Connecticut, but when he found he could not get exclusive rights to the Hartford stadium due to Association demands he threw in the sponge. So, ironically, professional soccer was launched in North America without the man who had done much to sustain it since 1960.

The National Professional Soccer League decided to strike out boldly by fielding teams in 1967. This threw expensive sand into the gears of the rival United Soccer Association, which had envisioned a 1968 launching. Rather than leave the field to the National League, the Association improvised a mini-schedule for 1967 using intact teams from Europe and South America which could readily be brought over with FIFA approval.

Soon merger talks between the two leagues got started but thorny personality and financial problems cropped up. When the National League demanded recognition from the United States Soccer Football Association this organization politely suggested that the League and the United Soccer Association reach some kind of agreement among themselves without involving the governing body.

Although the League offered to meet the stiff terms laid down by the United States Soccer Football Association—each club to pay a franchise fee of $25,000 plus four percent of the gate and ten percent of television receipts—the offer was turned down.

The governing body was in a legal dilemma. If the United States Soccer Football Association recognized the National Professional Soccer League and welcomed it thereby into world soccer, could not the United Soccer Association institute suit for damages on the grounds its exclusive contract had been violated?

If, on the other hand, the Association refused to recognize the League, could not the League bring action under the anti-trust laws? The courts have long taken a dim view of any restrictive action that deprives a man of the right to do business where he wishes. American professional sports generally, starting with baseball, have existed in a kind of legal no-man's-land with assorted terrors lurking around every corner.

Early in September of 1967 it looked as if a merger was ready to be signed and sealed. As Commissioner Macker said, "only the fine print remains to be discussed." But unexpected, stubborn snags arose, chiefly in the six cities where the two leagues each had a team. The merger talks collapsed.

On September 9, 1967, one day following the breakup of the

11

Chicago merger talks, the National Professional Soccer League took its complaint to court. An $18,000,000 action was filed in the Southern District Federal Court of New York under the antitrust laws against the United States Soccer Football Association, the United Soccer Association, and the Federation Internationale de Football Associations charging a conspiracy to drive the League out of business. The League claimed the three organizations made a contract giving the United Soccer Association exclusive control for ten years over professional soccer in the United States, and that thereby the League had been unjustly branded as outlaw. Said Commissioner Macker:

"The intent of this suit simply is to ask the court who are the outlaws under the Sherman Act, to secure an injunction which will reform this legal monopoly and to be awarded recompense suffered by NPSL members. It is generally known that the NPSL made this decision only after months of fruitless efforts to gain official sanction from the USSFA on the same terms and conditions as agreed to by the USA, excluding, of course, only the ten year monopoly provision under which only USA teams would be recognized by organized soccer."

As for the birth of the USA, the suit charged:

"USSFA's sub-committee, which had been appointed by USSFA's president, Frank Woods, and consisted of James McGuire, chairman, Erwin Single and Jack Flamhaft, recommended to USSFA's annual meeting held on June 25 and 26, 1966, that United be given exclusive recognition and this recommendation was adopted at the annual meeting. James McGuire was then immediately elected president of United and is its president at the present time. Mr. Frank Woods has accepted employment with the holder of the San Francisco franchise of United. Other persons connected with the USSFA have received direct and lucrative benefits because of USSFA's exclusive recognition of United."

McGuire's salary from the United Soccer Association is reputed to be about $25,000 yearly.

12

The suit went on to say that "in exchange for exclusive recognition, United has agreed to make certain contributions to USSFA which vastly exceed any sums of money that USSFA has ever previously exacted from any association or league in exchange for recognition. Under the agreement each League member is required to pay $25,000 to the Association for its franchise, or a total of $250,000. In addition the League is required to pay USSFA 4 percent of the gross ticket receipts of each league game (after deducting all admission taxes and 17½ percent of such gross receipts to cover stadium rental) and 5 percent of such receipts from each International Club Game and each Tour Game. The League is also required to pay USSFA 10 percent of all revenues received by the League under contracts providing for national radio and television coverage of League, Tour, and International Club games, but such percentage shall not exceed $150,000 in any one year. The agreement is to run for an initial period of ten years with rights of renewal. USSFA's total assets are approximately $40,000 and its annual budget has heretofore been less than $80,000. The vast sums agreed to be paid by United to USSFA are solely in exchange for the exercise of USSFA's monopoly power in the United States as a member of FIFA to grant exclusive recognition to United and effectively to exclude the plaintiffs from organized soccer throughout the world."

The English Football Association soon entered the fray. It set in motion suspensions for one year against six players who returned home after a season in the National Professional Soccer League. The London press generally took a sympathetic view of the players' plight, and quoted Clive Toye of the Baltimore Bays—who planned to return to Baltimore in 1968 anyway —as saying:

"I'm surprised at the F.A. It's not as though we are doing football any harm. Indeed, we are doing it a great deal of good. We now have 35,000 boys interested in soccer and not one of

13

them had kicked a ball before we started up in Baltimore. That has been done for the game and not for gain."

The sports world trembled, including owners of teams in baseball, football, and basketball. Everyone agrees that professional sports must have a responsible, well-defined structure. But laws and court decisions on the form this structure should take, including the right of individual players to negotiate directly for their services without being bound irrevocably to one club, have been virtually nonexistent. By one means or another, professional sports has generally managed to stay out of court. After World War II Danny Gardella, a minor player for the New York Giants, jumped to the Mexican League and was blacklisted on his return. He sued, lost in Federal circuit court, and then in 1949 won a surprising 2–1 decision in the district court of appeals. Baseball wanted no more of the case and settled for $60,000. Now the suit by the National Professional Soccer League appeared to have opened a Pandora's box of legal vexations.

Long before the League moved its fight into the courthouse, FIFA and its international president, Sir Stanley Rous of England, had been dismayed by the internecine warfare in the richest nation in the world, the one on which professional soccer had long set covetous eyes. Yet through it all Sir Stanley remained stubbornly optimistic, feeling that somehow the damage could be repaired.

"The only problem exists in cities such as New York, Los Angeles, Chicago, Toronto, Boston and the San Francisco area where there are two clubs," he said. "As for players who left their clubs to join what you might term the outlaw league, a settlement can be reached here, too. We had this trouble in Colombia and Australia on a heavier scale. In Australia, FIFA acted as a referee on claims of the clubs that lost players to the outlaws. If they asked too much we whittled it down. Some, of course, were hardly worth the outlandish prices their old clubs sought. As for raiding teams for players, British teams have been doing it for years. English teams are always chasing Scottish players. Now the Scots are after the Swedes and Italy and Spain are after everybody else."

Despite FIFA's eagerness to be impartial and to bring about peace in North American soccer, it was necessary to intervene when the National Professional Soccer League arranged for Atletico Portuguesa of Brazil to play the New York Generals at Yankee Stadium in the summer of 1967. At first it appeared that the Brazilian team might defy any ban imposed by FIFA but twenty-six hours before the scheduled kickoff the game was canceled. Commissioner Macker was bitter. He called the cancellation "another step in the stifling of the development of soccer in the United States. It is obvious the pressure became just too much for the team to bear. It came both from FIFA and the Brazilian Confederation of Sport. However, I feel they should have gone ahead with the contest since they had signed a valid contract and the Generals had undertaken expenses. The action of FIFA is disgraceful."

Dr. Helmut Kaeser, secretary-general of FIFA, acknowledged that both the Brazilian Confederation of Sport and Atletico Portuguesa had been warned that the match was not permissible: "FIFA regulations strictly forbid any club to play against an unaffiliated team."

However, in a strange twist possible only in the wonderland of sport, the United States Soccer Football Association in the autumn of 1967 gave permission to all players of what it then considered the outlaw National Professional Soccer League to play for sanctioned clubs in the long-established, semiprofessional American League. Many NPSL players took advantage of the opportunity in the off-season.

Long before the alphabetical battle lines were drawn between FIFA, USSFA, USA, and NPSL, Bill MacPhail, Columbia Broadcasting System vice-president in charge of sports, was an interested spectator to soccer's growing pains. He had weighed the game's television potential for two years and thought it had a great chance in the United States and Canada. Aware that several years of development were still needed, he none the less decided at an early date to get into it.

"We waited as long as we could, hoping the two leagues would get together, and did everything possible to effect a merger," said MacPhail. "Finally we decided on the National Professional Soccer League for two reasons: 1—It planned to start a year before the other league with its own teams; and 2—I saw the contracts with the clubs and the stadiums and knew it [the League] was solid."

Bob Hermann, president of the League, later revealed each of his teams put up a $250,000 performance bond. Any team that collapsed in midseason would have forfeited this to C.B.S. The network was thus safe in offering a soccer game every Sunday—attractions, said Hermann, that drew an average of 10,000,000 viewers each week. C.B.S. renewed its contract with the League for 1968 and then expanded the coverage to include all the teams in the merger. MacPhail termed himself "delighted" with the contract renewal and said, "The initial season saw the development of a high quality of major league play."

Commissioner Macker peered hopefully into the future: "Soccer is one sport which eventually will be adaptable to the tremendous opportunities offered by global television. When teams of the National Professional Soccer League are permitted by organized soccer to play the top teams of the world, it is not difficult to envision the reception which telecasts of the game will have in London, Rome, Paris, Buenos Aires or other population centers where the sport is so popular today."

At the time the TV contract was a big boost to the NPSL and a hard blow to the pocketbook and prestige of the USA. Under the agreement, C.B.S. would pay the NPSL $500,000 the first year, $700,000 the second, and then $900,000, $1,100,000, $1,300,000, $1,500,000, and $2,000,000 for the succeeding years.

So, contrary to the popular impression that television created a soccer league for the edification of its audiences, both the

NPSL and the USA came first. NPSL's TV contract, therefore, was an outgrowth, undeniably lucrative, of the League's formation.

The United Soccer Association was not long deterred by the loss of the TV contract or by the speedy action of its rival in deciding to field teams in 1967. Rather, it countered with hand-picked team imports and soon boasted that its level of play was higher, and its average crowd larger, than in the NPSL. Nevertheless it still faced a major problem: in 1968 it would need to start the team-building task that the NPSL began in 1967, a task complicated by the fact that each of the clubs could spend no more than $200,000 in transfer fees (soccer's term for the purchase of a player by one club from another) and that each team must sign an increasing number of native American and Canadian players.

The NPSL acted quickly in the autumn of 1966 and winter of 1967 to put together teams of players, most of whose contracts with foreign teams had expired. FIFA rules require such players to negotiate first with their own clubs. This requirement is almost as rigid as baseball's reserve clause, which prevents a baseball player from striking out on his own when he is unhappy with the terms offered him. In many cases NPSL clubs acquired soccer players outright by payment to the players' clubs of fees as high as $25,000. Some players reported they were told that if they signed with the NPSL at what by European standards were very lush salaries indeed they would face a suspension of only six months in case the venture failed and they wished to return. Later, obviously, FIFA decided to double the punishment.

"We don't think there is anything morally or legally wrong with signing a player whose contract has expired," said John Pinto, president of NPSL's New York Generals. "It's the same in professional football. Once a man plays out his option, he is a free agent."

"Outlaws . . . rebels," shrieked the European press. Some foreign players refused to deal with NPSL clubs. Others, satisfied that payment of the transfer fee or its equivalent had cleared the way, or perhaps feeling they were nearing the end of their careers, were enticed by contracts that ran up to $25,000 yearly. The NPSL also signed American players and outstanding foreign amateurs.

European professional soccer players average about $100 per week. No wonder some foreign stars shrugged off the threat of possible banishment by FIFA with the salty observation that "since we have been paid peanuts for playing soccer in England, let's get some dollars for a change."

The International Federation of Professional Footballers, which has 50,000 members, bestowed its blessing on the unsanctioned NPSL: "We welcome the start of the NPSL and are happy to recognize them; we are happy at the opportunity afforded our members to play in the NPSL."

The two leagues, although joined in a courtroom battle, refrained from name-calling and seemed to be conditioning themselves for coexistence.

Commissioner Walsh of the United Soccer Association, with his baseball background, remarked, "I'm accustomed to the idea of living with two leagues."

"There is room on the North American continent for more than one league," said President Robert Hermann of the NPSL. "In fact, we need two leagues. It makes for competition and is good for soccer. That's our main aim—to promote soccer in the United States and Canada."

Once the franchise lines had been drawn, the two leagues promptly found commissioners, men of solid reputation. They became recipients of substantial contracts. The backers of soccer knew full well the importance of competent executive direction at the top.

The United Soccer Association chose 41-year-old Richard B. Walsh, Jr., of Los Angeles. Walsh started with the Dodger baseball organization in 1949 and rose to vice-president and assistant general manager. Admitting he picked up his knowledge of soccer as he went along, Walsh soon termed it: "Much more exciting than baseball . . . and the spectators will know for sure that every game is less than two hours long, an hour and a half of which is constant action, plus an intermission between halves."

The National Professional Soccer League picked Ken Macker, fifty, a man with solid experience in both communications and sports. He came to the job after six years in Manila as publisher of three daily newspapers and president of a twelve-station television and radio network. In 1955 and 1956 Macker and his partner Pete Rozelle of professional football fame were hired by the city of Melbourne to promote the 1956 Olympic Games, then withering under the criticism of the Olympic president, Avery Brundage. They did the job so well the Games were staged with great success.

But if the two professional soccer leagues took an entirely different approach to FIFA and to the recruiting of teams and players, they had one practice in common. Each team was headed by wealthy men well seasoned in sports promotion. These were no tyros in the art of luring people through turnstiles. Nor were they starry-eyed visionaries who expected vast crowds and fast profits at the very outset. They knew they were in for a hard pull.

"Our backers conducted very extensive market research studies to see what the potential was," said Macker. "The prediction was made it would take soccer three to five years to catch on. It took professional football generations."

"The owners have gone into this with their eyes open," said Walsh. "They know what it takes to build from the ground floor."

For 1967 the United Soccer Association lined up as follows:

Boston, represented by the Shamrock Rovers of Dublin, Ireland.

Chicago, represented by Cagliari of Sardinia, Italy, and including among its backers John W. Allyn of the Chicago White Sox.

Cleveland, represented by the Stoke City Potters of Stoke-on-Trent, England, and numbering Gabe Paul of the Cleveland Indians as a backer.

Dallas, represented by Dundee United of Dundee, Scotland, with Lamar Hunt of the famous oil family among the sponsors.

Detroit, represented by Glentoran of Belfast, Northern Ireland, and backed among others by John W. Anderson II and William Clay Ford.

Houston, represented by Bangu of Rio de Janeiro, Brazil, and backed by Judge Roy Hofheinz of the Astrodome.

Los Angeles, represented by the Wolverhampton Wanderers of Wolverhampton, England, and backed by Jack Kent Cooke.

New York, represented by Cerro of Montevideo, Uruguay, and backed by Madison Square Garden.

San Francisco, represented by A.D.O. of The Hague, Holland. A.D.O. are the initials of the Dutch phrase, *Alles Door Oefening*, "Everything Through Endeavor."

Toronto, represented by Hibernian of Edinburgh, Scotland.

Vancouver, represented by Sunderland of Sunderland, England, with Brigadier General E. G. Eakins one of the backers.

Washington, represented by the Aberdeen Dons of Aberdeen, Scotland.

For championship play-off purposes, the league was divided into two divisions: Eastern—Boston Shamrock Rovers, Cleveland Stokers, Detroit Cougars, New York Skyliners, Toronto City, and the Washington Whips; Western—Chicago Mustangs, Dallas Tornadoes, Houston Stars, Los Angeles Wolves, San Francisco Golden Gate Gales, and the Vancouver Royal Canadians.

On the other side of the fence was the National Professional Soccer League with individually recruited teams that lined up this way:

Boston, a charter member which did not play in 1967, backed

by a syndicate that included Richard O'Connell of the Boston baseball Red Sox and Arnold (Red) Auerbach of the Boston basketball Celtics.

Atlanta, backed by William Bartholomay of the Atlanta baseball Braves, among others.

Baltimore, owned by Jerold Hoffberger of the Baltimore baseball Orioles.

Chicago, owned by William B. Cutler, investment broker, and Al Kaczmarek, a businessman long associated with soccer.

Los Angeles, backed by Dan Martin, former Undersecretary of Commerce, and Dan Reeves of the Los Angeles football Rams.

New York, backed by RKO-General, John Pinto, and Peter Elser, New York investment broker.

Philadelphia, backed by John J. Rooney of the Pittsburgh football Steelers and Gerald Lawrence.

Pittsburgh, backed by a syndicate headed by Richard George.

St. Louis, backed by a syndicate headed by Robert Hermann and William Bidwell of the St. Louis football Cardinals.

Oakland (San Francisco and Oakland) backed by H. T. Hilliard and Joe O'Neill, co-owners.

Toronto, owned by Joseph Peters, a real-estate tycoon.

The NPSL also had two divisions for championship purposes: Eastern—Pittsburgh Phantoms, Baltimore Bays, Atlanta Chiefs, Philadelphia Spartans, and New York Generals; Western—St. Louis Stars, California Clippers, Los Angeles Toros, Chicago Spurs, and Toronto Falcons.

As can be seen there were rival soccer teams in Chicago, Los Angeles, New York, Boston, San Francisco–Oakland, and Toronto.

The question "Will soccer really succeed in the United States and Canada?" persisted.

Early in the century, Frank Bucklet, manager of the Wolves, a famous English team at a time when Britain completely dominated the game, predicted that the time would come

21

when European countries would develop great players—which they certainly did along with Latin America—"but we ought to look out for the day when the United States takes up the game seriously."

He was thinking, of course, that American athletes with their fiercely competitive attitude might come to dominate soccer just as they took over such once exclusively British sports as golf, boxing, and tennis.

Brian Glanville of the *Sunday Times* of London, while taking a rather jaundiced view of the 1967 soccer season in North America, remained cautiously optimistic: "Yet there *are* substantial hopes, and these center in an eventual interaction between the spread of soccer in the schools, and improvement at the professional level."

Both leagues felt the same way, and worked hard in each city with clinics and coaching sessions for schoolboys.

It seems appropriate now to take a closer look at the two soccer events of 1966 that had tremendous impact on American sports followers.

On July 30 the final of the World Cup, the four-year pinnacle of professional soccer, was televised live by satellite and by direct circuits throughout Europe to a world audience estimated at 400,000,000, not a few million of which were Canadians and Americans. The reaction was enthusiastic. Many newspapers on this side of the Atlantic gave bigger headlines to the game than they did to the baseball games and horse races of that day.

A better match could scarcely have been found to display soccer impressively to Canada and the United States. England had never won the World Cup since the international competition started in 1930, and soccer was England's own, special game. Now the finals brought together England and West Germany before 100,000 in Wembley Stadium including the Queen and most of the royal family.

Germany scored first after ten minutes of play. England tied

22

it ten minutes later at 1–1 and went ahead 2–1 ten minutes before the end of the game. With only seconds left to play Wolfgang Weber, in a skirmish in front of the English goal, tied the game at 2–2. That forced it into thirty minutes of overtime. It should be explained that overtime is never used in ordinary soccer games but only at the championship level. England finally won 4–2 in a game that paced so furiously that Gary Rosenthal, dean of students at Long Island University's Brooklyn Center and a soccer coach himself, wrote in *The New York Times* that "the immediate impression made by the greatest soccer players in the world is that their physical condition is superb . . . the players were playing nearly as hard at the end of the overtime as they had all the game." And it might be added that there were no substitutions.

Try to evaluate what follows, in view of the fact that in many American sports delaying tactics are considered standard procedure for a team that is leading by a slender margin. W. Granger Blair, in his story of the game itself in *The Times*, wrote: "Only once did the English team stall—about three minutes before the end of regulation play. The crowd began booing and the home eleven quickly swung back to the offensive, thereby giving the West Germans their golden opportunity."

The televised game started North American sports fans talking soccer. The second augury of success followed soon after when a crowd of 41,598, the largest ever to see a soccer game in the United States or Canada, thronged into Yankee Stadium on Labor Day of 1966. It had come to see the two best teams and the greatest soccer player in the world. Inter of Milan held the world club title for the two previous years. Santos of Brazil held it the preceding two years. And Santos had the one and only Pelé.

As happens in almost every game he plays, Pelé was tripped and mauled in the Brazilians' 4–1 rout of Inter and he lost two goals because of off-sides. But the one he did make was spec-

23

tacular. Taking the ball in front of the goal he dribbled to his right (dribbling is done with the feet, not hands, in soccer) drawing a defender with him, and then suddenly raced ahead and drove the ball into the nets to the dismay of the predominantly pro-Italian audience.

Then early in 1967 occurred probably the most amazing of all soccer manifestations. In Houston's Astrodome, Real Madrid and West Ham United drew a crowd of 33,351. At the end the spectators, many of whom had never seen a soccer game before, rose to their feet for a long, loud ovation.

It was, no doubt, acclaim for two fine teams. It was also acclaim for the game of soccer.

3

The merger of the two leagues and worldwide acceptance of American professional soccer

———◆———

All sensible men connected with soccer in North America recognized there could be no hope for the game unless the United Soccer Association and the National Professional Soccer League merged, and the United States and Canadian Soccer Football Associations—and of course FIFA—gave their blessing to the marriage. It was manifestly absurd to have two teams in cities that had difficulty supporting one. The two national soccer associations were in a perilous position with the NPSL's $18,000,000 antitrust suit hanging over their heads. The NPSL was operating in a twilight zone without official recognition.

The financial losses were heavy on all sides. One soccer executive estimated that National Professional Soccer League teams lost between $600,000 and $800,000 each in 1967, and United Soccer Association teams lost between $200,000 and $300,000 each. The USA was lucky. It had a shorter season.

Time and again it seemed as if the merger was about to be

accomplished but always at the last minute new obstacles cropped up.

Finally in the waning days of 1967 Sir Stanley Rous, president of FIFA, took decisive action. He sent a telegram to the warring factions which said: "Unless litigation in New York settled by Dec. 15 on basis of FIFA's well established policy that national associations accept on equal terms all clubs who are willing to comply with world football principles, FIFA emergency committee will consider on Dec. 20 where USSFA has violated above policy. Failure to do so will certainly result in a vote for suspension of USSFA."

Suspension of USSFA and presumably of the Canadian association as well would mean that all soccer in the United States and Canada, amateur and professional, NPSL as well as USA, would be cast into the limbo of nonrecognition. Carried to its ultimate limit this would bar the visits of foreign teams, stop the importation of foreign stars, and even prevent the participation of the United States and Canada in the soccer tournament of the Olympic Games.

The contending soccer promoters met in Chicago in the Drake Hotel December 12 and 13 and ironed out virtually all the merger details barely under Sir Stanley's deadline. Walsh and Macker, who had always favored a merger, accompanied by Bob Guelker, president of USSFA, reported the good news to Sir Stanley in FIFA House in Zurich, Switzerland, December 16.

The public announcement came when the two rival leagues met in New York January 4 and 5 of 1968 and the wedding took place with little evidence of a shotgun in the background. The $18,000,000 antitrust suit was quietly buried. For twenty-four hours the happy pair was known as the Professional Soccer League. Then this rather colorless monicker was quickly changed to North American Soccer League, the name the United Soccer Association had originally adopted, the one which had been in Bill Cox's mind when he first dreamed of introducing soccer on a broad scale in the United States and Canada.

At first it was proposed that the two leagues continue to operate separately; or, as Tom Reynolds, former NPSL counsel and a part owner of the Atlanta Chiefs, put it, "We thought it would be best to get everybody in the bedroom first before we got into bed together." But the owners decided on immediate union. The teams of the two leagues were thoroughly scrambled and then divided on a geographical basis. Macker became President of the Western Conference and Walsh of the Eastern. Presiding over both was an executive committee with John Anderson of the Detroit Cougars (USA) as chairman, Joseph O'Neill of the Oakland Clippers (NPSL) as deputy chairman, and Bob Hermann of the St. Louis Stars (NPSL) and John Allyn of the Chicago Mustangs (USA) as committee members.

The problem of the six cities that had duplicate teams was solved this way:

San Francisco—Even before the merger was accomplished, the San Francisco Gales (USA) joined forces with the Vancouver Royals (USA), moving out of the Bay area and taking with them their famous player-coach, Ferenc Puskas. This left the field to the Oakland Clippers (NPSL).

New York—Both Madison Square Garden, which had sponsored the Skyliners in the USA, and RKO-General, backer of the Generals in the NPSL, withdrew. The single New York franchise was awarded to Peter Elser, a New York investment broker with a high enthusiasm for soccer. Elser had a forty-five percent interest in the Generals. He decided to retain this name for the New York team, as well as its British coach, Fred Goodwin.

Chicago—The Spurs (NPSL) moved to Kansas City, leaving Allyn's Mustangs (USA) as sole team in the city. With the Spurs went their general manager, Al Kaczmarek. John Latshaw and George Powell, Kansas City businessmen, took over sponsorship.

Los Angeles—The Toros of the NPSL moved to San Diego where Bill Cox had an interest. It seemed only poetic justice for him to be back in the picture. Jack Kent Cooke's Wolves (USA) had Los Angeles to themselves.

Boston—The United Soccer Association club accepted compensation from the NPSL team and disbanded.

Toronto—The Toronto City owner, Steve Stavro, was paid $160,000 to give up his USA franchise and the NPSL club was left alone in the Canadian metropolis.

In addition to these shifts and mergers, two 1967 NPSL clubs dropped out: Pittsburgh, which had troubles all season, and, oddly enough, Philadelphia, which probably has more indigenous soccer than any other city in North America (except possibly St. Louis).

The two conferences were divided into two divisions each for play-off purposes and to build natural rivalries. Dick Walsh's Eastern Conference lined up this way:

Atlantic Division—Atlanta (NPSL), Baltimore (NPSL), Boston (NPSL), New York (NPSL–USA), and Washington (USA).

Lakes Division—Cleveland (USA), Chicago (USA), Detroit (USA), and Toronto (NPSL).

In the Western Conference presided over by Ken Macker the teams were divided thus:

Pacific Division—Vancouver (USA), Oakland (NPSL), Los Angeles (USA), and San Diego (NPSL).

Gulf Division—Houston (USA), Dallas (USA), Kansas City (NPSL), and St. Louis (NPSL).

The United States Soccer Football Association gratefully accepted the $25,000 entry fees of the former NPSL teams, a new contract embracing all teams in both conferences was negotiated with the Columbia Broadcasting System, and soccer's bright, new tomorrow dawned.

4

The Americanization of the game of soccer

———◆———

Almost everywhere in the world "Americanization" is a nasty word used to describe the spread of a way of life that other nations profess to scorn even as they make haste to adopt it. Along with the physical aspects—supermarkets, hot dogs, elaborate plumbing, air conditioning, lunch counters, precooked meals, soft drinks, tin cans, and a great variety of gadgets—there comes a sense of speed. Americans are always in a hurry. Comic-strip language comes to mind: "Boom! Zip! Bang! Zing! Biff! . . ."

If soccer, English in origin, worldwide in acceptance, and already a very fast game, becomes popular in North America will it not undergo Americanization and perhaps be Canadianized as well?

The answer must be a qualified "Yes."

Even before the 1967 season started, the National Professional Soccer League made a change in the traditional point-standings system in order to put more punch into the offensive side of the game. As games were televised, arbitrary stoppages in the flow of play were considered to provide time for commercial messages, a problem not smoothed out without much hue and cry. Players' names began to appear on uniforms, as is common in baseball and football; and in many cities soccer found a new setting in baseball stadiums. Surprisingly these stadiums accommodated soccer better than American football.

The Americanization of soccer was under way.

The device hit on by the National Professional Soccer League to put more zip, zing, boom and biff into the game was a simple one. Traditionally in soccer two points are awarded for a victory and one for a tie in the league standings that determine the championships. With this system teams became content to play for a tie in games on the road, win a good share of those at home, where they had the advantage of a friendly crowd and a familiar field, and thus take the league title through defensive play.

The NPSL decided to award six points for a victory and three for a tie, with the added proviso that every goal scored up to and including three on a side also counts for a point. This meant that a winning team could pick up nine points in a game and a losing team three. It also meant that when a team was trailing in a hopeless score in soccer, such as 4–0, there would still be a strong incentive for the losers to try their utmost to score a goal or two.

Americans and Canadians like keeping score. They also like the thrill that goes with goals, touchdowns, baskets, runs. The NPSL change was designed to encourage scoring in a sport notorious for its large number of scoreless or low-score games, and notorious, too, in recent years, for an increasing emphasis on defensive action in play.

The scoring in American-style football has been opened up by the professionals, making 37–34 games almost commonplace; the scoring in basketball has become so energized that a team incapable of scoring 100 points in a game is felt to be impotent; why couldn't the scoring in soccer be improved?

If a 37–34 football game is an improvement on 6–0, and a 125–119 basketball game more exciting than 17–15, then might not a 7–6 soccer game or even 10–8 set pulses going faster than 1–0, or worst of all, 0–0.

The United Soccer Association, however, sided with tradition. It held to two points for a victory and one for a tie. When the two leagues merged it was decided, after considerable debate, to adopt the energized NPSL point system.

But neither league could escape the Americanizing effect of television.

On a black-and-white television screen the standard black shirt and shorts of the referee look like those of any player in dark attire. In football, baseball, hockey, and basketball the uniforms of the players are so characteristic that they could not possibly be confused with officials. But soccer players wear jerseys and shorts and no padding whatsoever.

So to avoid confusion, NPSL referees donned black-and-white-striped shirts that set them apart from the contestants.

The next innovation the NPSL considered was a warning gun fired two minutes before the end of the half and two minutes before the end of the game. Hitherto both spectators and players were kept in the dark as to the progress of time and could only surmise when play would end. The referee kept his watch carefully screened from all observers and suddenly blew a whistle to terminate matters. The countdown clocks on electric scoreboards were put into use instead, solving everything without a gun. The suspense that builds near the end of a close game was now underscored.

Television produced another problem of quite a different character.

The owners of soccer teams looked on television as the key to open the door to riches. The direct revenues it brings are certainly substantial. But television also builds fan support. The

National Football League, with its artful televising of road games but not of home games, provided a shining example of how the electronic camera could create an almost hysterical demand for tickets. But how was the game of soccer, in which interruptions are rare and usually very brief, going to provide the breaks needed for commercials without impeding the action?

Commercials are no problem in baseball, with the leisurely exchange of fields each half-inning, nor in boxing, where there is a one-minute break between rounds.

Providing for commercials in TV football, however, is more difficult, despite the time-outs that the teams themselves call. Officials have sometimes needed to stop both professional and college games to get in television advertisements. When this happens at critical moments a team's momentum can be destroyed.

Arranging for commercials in soccer, as well as in hockey, was a gigantic headache until the use of one of the wonders of modern electronics provided a satisfactory means.

Soccer is played in two furious halves of forty-five minutes each, during which time the only occasions for the interruption of action—and all of these are usually very brief—are a serious injury to a player; a throw-in after the ball has been kicked over the sidelines; or when the ball goes over the goal line but not into the goal net, in which case it is kicked back into play from a corner of the field or from the goal area, depending on which team touched it last; or, finally, when a goal has been scored and play is started from the center of the field.

But with a hustling team the interruption of play can be brief, except when an injured player must be taken from the field.

Commissioner Macker of the NPSL, which was happy with a C.B.S. TV contract, put it this way before the season started:

"Let's face it. With television we must have time-outs for commercials. There will be fourteen to a game—five in each half, and the balance before we start, between halves, or at the end. But we won't break into the game and disturb its fluidity.

"When the ball goes out of bounds, which happens a dozen or so times, it is calculated it takes forty seconds to put it back into play. We will prolong this for one minute."

But alas for theory. The 1967 season of the NPSL was scarcely under way when an incident occurred which was seized on ferociously by detractors of the game but in the end served to clear the atmosphere.

Peter Rhodes, one of England's outstanding referees and a man of unquestioned integrity, was reported in Toronto as saying that of twenty-one fouls he called in a televised game, eleven were "phonies" to permit C.B.S. to work in commercials.

He promptly denied saying anything of the kind but admitted with complete candor that he had held slightly injured players on the ground long enough to get in the desired commercial. In one particularly flagrant instance, Co Prins, the Pittsburgh captain and playing coach, slipped in the middle of the field. When he tried to jump to his feet, Rhodes pushed him down and the commercial went on.

"I have a small radio receiver unit strapped on my back for televised games," Rhodes explained. "I get three beeps and I hear a producer saying, 'A commercial is coming up,' so I have to get play stopped.

"But eleven false fouls is complete nonsense. I did not call any false fouls. It would violate the Laws of the game and would be dishonest and unfair to the players. A foul means a free kick, which could land in the goal area."

Then Commissioner Macker spoke out:

"The NPSL has been experimenting for several weeks with methods of providing time for commercials required for TV sponsors of our game.

"The incident at Toronto involving Peter Rhodes has crystallized our thinking regarding this matter.

"All time-outs called by the referee to accommodate such TV

commercials will be clearly indicated by the referee for the information of both the spectators and the TV audience."

The referee, it was decided, would wave a red handkerchief over his head when he was calling time for a TV commercial and this would be done only after goals, goal kicks, injuries that require a trainer's attention, and before corner kicks and side-line throw-ins.

But even this system did not work smoothly. So television dug further into its bag of tricks and came up with the perfect answer. Commercials would be inserted only during natural pauses in the game and play would be allowed to resume as speedily as possible. Any action that occurred while the com-mercial was still on would be recorded on electronic tape and played back if significant or exciting. This, in fact, was the same device that the rival United Soccer Association, which in 1967 was covered only on local television, had already decided on.

Commissioner Walsh of the USA had decreed that "commer-cials will be inserted only after the offensive team kicks the ball over the goal line, thus setting up a goal kick by the defensive team. The game will continue uninterrupted with the TV sta-tion putting any missed action on tape to show later if anything important should transpire. There will be no communication whatsoever between the referee or linesman and the producers. In other words, no two-way radios, no red flags, no red caps."

However, after the dust stirred up by the Rhodes incident had settled, there came the sober realization that television and sport are intimately and intricately laced together.

As Milt Dunnell wrote in the Toronto *Daily Star* after the Rhodes incident:

"Television is a demanding sugar daddy. Most professional sports have put themselves in the position where they could not live without its millions. To get these millions, sport has to give back something. The sponsor who pays $70,000 a minute to advertise his fingernail polish during a National Football

League game regards those 60 seconds as the most important in the whole day."

And Dick Young, in the New York *News,* in a column formerly critical of the handling of soccer commercials, said: "There is nothing wrong with calling a few time-outs for the purpose of getting in TV commercials. After all, you take the money from the detergent manufacturer and he is entitled to get his message across. All that is asked by any reasonable person is that good judgment be used."

But how about the Americanization of stadiums?

To date there are no soccer stadiums in the United States or Canada, and those North Americans who somehow manage to believe that everything they have is bigger and better than can be found anywhere else would be startled to see the new and ultramodern 100,000-seat soccer stadium in Mexico City and the cluster of similar-sized giants throughout South America. The big daddy of them all is Rio de Janeiro's 200,000-seat goliath.

Although literally millions of soccer games have been played in the United States and Canada in the last century, most have been in open fields with a few hundred spectators clustered around the edges or, at best, in small stadiums.

Fortunately for the soccer promoters, baseball stadiums, while for the most part poorly adapted to professional football because of the vast distance between most spectators and the long and narrow playing field, are ideal for soccer, as are many of the older football stadiums. Football is played on a field 100 yards long and 53.1 yards wide. The international rules of soccer call for a field not more than 120 yards long nor less than 110, and not more than 80 yards wide nor less than 70. The soccer field in Yankee Stadium, for instance, is 115 yards by 77 yards and that means that there is much more action close to the stands than in professional football. Similarly, when soccer teams play in stadiums designed for football the gap between the stands and the field is much narrower than it is in the American-type game. It appears that the transplanting of soccer to stadiums intended for baseball or football has been the easiest of all steps in the Americanization of the game.

Holding soccer games in baseball parks does require the players to make some adjustments. In one corner of the baseball field there is apt to be the bare dirt of the infield. This can cause trouble for players accustomed to controlling the ball on turf and needing their highest skills as they approach the goal.

And the crowd is different, too. Unlike most baseball crowds and some football crowds, it stays to the very end because soccer games are almost invariably close. Getting out of a sizable soccer crowd at most stadiums is a far more formidable task than getting out of an even larger baseball crowd in the same park. The baseball crowd starts drifting out from the sixth inning on. Not so in soccer.

But if many external aspects of the game have been adapted to an American setting, the internal aspects have not. There is a togetherness about a soccer team that seems completely alien to American professional sports.

For one thing, in social contacts off the field players usually wear team blazers and ties—green, red, blue, yellow, the colors of their field uniform. They relax together much more than athletes in other sports. Three hours before a game they assemble in a restaurant for their pregame meal. Baseball and football players, by contrast, eat when and where they wish beforehand. For soccer players the pregame meal is almost prescribed: plain steak, toast, and tea. Italian, Spanish and Latin-American players substitute wine for tea. American professional football and baseball contracts specifically forbid alcoholic beverages as an expense-account item. For some soccer players for whom wine is a national mealtime habit, this would be a cruel and inhuman punishment.

When a soccer team assembles in the locker room to "suit up" the atmosphere is subdued, much less rowdy than in baseball or football, where loud talk of golf, girls, umpires, stocks and bonds, plus a sprinkling of practical jokes and horseplay are locker-room staples.

The pregame talk by the soccer coach is on a low key:

"Don't forget that tonight we're being watched. I want you to work hard helping each other, talking to each other, but keep composed. Play the ball on the left-hand side. That's their weakness. Try out the pitch when you get out there and judge how fast the ball is running. The game isn't over until the final whistle." (The "pitch," incidentally, is the turf, the field itself.)

Warm-ups before a game, as in baseball and football, are not necessary. In an average soccer game a player runs a total of seven to ten miles, and 2,000 yards of this at all-out sprinting speed. He gets warm enough as the game progresses.

An Americanism that is not yet popular with foreign players and may take longer to catch on is the custom of showering. Elsewhere in the world the entire team gets into one enormous tub and there they sit and talk for a half hour or more. They discuss the game, their mistakes, the good plays, and slowly the bruises and kicks fade away in the soothing water and the glow of comradeship.

Foreign players, dazzled as they are by the wall-to-wall carpeting, spacious cubicles and elaborate rubdown rooms found in America's baseball and football clubhouse quarters, would gladly trade it all for soccer's traditional big tub.

5

The history and the growth of soccer

———◆———

Why is it that the originally English game of soccer is played around the globe, in every civilized land (and in many that are not), and in most is considered the national sport, commonly drawing crowds of 100,000 in Europe and as vast as 200,000 in Brazil?

Yet American baseball, though it has been exported, too, has succeeded more narrowly, chiefly in Canada, Japan, Mexico and portions of Latin America.

And American football has been exported nowhere (except to Canada, where it underwent a change into a faster, more open game where kicking is a major factor).

Might it be that soccer is truly the universal game because it is fluid, fast, and easy to understand, and requires little of its players other than that they be agile, well-conditioned, and intelligent—with no premium given for being seven feet tall or weighing 300 pounds?

It is reasonable to believe that the combination of simplicity and excitement has indeed accounted for the spread of soccer.

The necessary equipment is inexpensive. The danger of serious injury is quite small. Boys can play it in backyards with no more than three or four on a team. An average-sized man or even a small one can rise to stardom in it. It is an adaptable, flexible game that lends itself to enjoyment all the way from children kicking a makeshift ball up to the glamour of a World Cup final.

How did it all begin?

Place a round object in front of a male, particularly a young male, and although wearing expensive and polished shoes, his impulse is to kick it. There is evidence that round balls were kicked by the Chinese three thousand years before the time of Christ. The Romans brought *harpastrum*—involving a ball and like all Roman pastimes, mightily bloody and rough—to England when they came as conquerers. There is a story that when the early British repelled some Danish invaders they used the skull of one of them for a form of soccer.

For centuries the Italians have had *calcio*, a game in which a round ball is kicked vigorously. It is still played by large and formless teams in the Piazza della Signoria in Florence on the first Sunday in May and on the feast of St. John the Baptist.

And in Britain during at least the last 1,000 years rudimentary soccer has been a village sport, between villages, within villages, and up and down the countryside. In Derby, on Shrove Tuesday, teams numbering as many as five hundred to a side played between goal lines set up at Nun's Mill and Gallows' Balk, cracking heads, windows, and doors in glorious abandon. A politer form of the sport exists there today.

Soon the establishment came to look with disfavor on this violent and destructive sport. There were altogether too many coroners' reports and postmortems to please the authorities. Kings thundered against it. That they had to keep on thundering might indicate that kicking a ball can no more be legislated away than sex.

In 1314 Edward II forbade football in any form "For as much

as there is great noise in the city by hustling over large balls
... from which many evils might arise."

In 1349 Edward III enjoined it because it hampered archery.

In 1389 Richard II broadened the injunction and banned all
"playing at tennise, football and other games called corts...."

In 1401 Henry IV prohibited it.

In 1457 James III of Scotland lumped it with that other pernicious evil when he ordered that "football and golfe be utterly
cryed down and not to be used."

In 1491, his successor James IV issued a new statute that
decreed that "in na place of realme ther be used football, golfe,
or other sik unprofitable sports" but by 1497 his own high
treasurer paid two shillings for "fut balles," so perhaps in the
hardy north the royal prejudice was weakening.

But not so in London. In 1572 Queen Elizabeth decreed that
"no foteballe play be used or suffered within the city of
London and the liberties thereof upon pain of punishment."

However Oliver Cromwell was a football player and refers
to it in his letters and William Shakespeare took note of it in
A Comedy of Errors:

> Am I so round with you as you with me
> That like a football do you spurn me thus?

The next we know is that Charles II, a rather gay and dissolute monarch, it must be admitted, attended a match between
his servants and those of the Duke of Albemarle.

It must be clear from all this evidence that soccer was a sport
of the common man, at first scorned by royalty and legislated
against, then finally accepted.

Slowly soccer became respectable. Now it is eminently so.
The Football Association which governs English soccer in all
its forms, professional and amateur, college and schoolboy, has
as its patron the Queen, and its president is the Duke of
Gloucester. Field Marshal Viscount Montgomery is a vice-president. It is as though the President of the United States

presided over baseball from the major leagues down to the sandlots.

Soccer as we know it today did not take form until around 1800 and was still held in low esteem until the period of "muscular Christianity" came to England in the 1850's. Then the status-saturated public schools (in America known as "private") took soccer off the streets, and aided and abetted by the prestigious universities Oxford and Cambridge, drew up rules and made the game manly, respectable, and quite, quite proper. And the common man still loved it.

Obviously in the early part of the nineteenth century some kind of rules existed for soccer, although none are preserved in written form. The kicking features of the game had always been emphasized, from medieval times on, with a strict prohibition on carrying the ball. (In 1823 William Ellis, a Rugby schoolboy, started the game that became known as Rugby and eventually led to American-style football when he picked up a soccer ball and ran with it, as the Rugby monument says, "with a fine disregard of the rules of football.")

J. C. Thring drew up the ten fundamental rules of modern soccer in 1862, but the game's formal birthdate is October 26, 1863, when the Football Association was formed in Freemason's Tavern, Great Green Street, Lincoln Inn's Fields, London.

The very word "soccer" is a shortened form of "Association" —the sort of transmutation that the British are quite adept at— witness the pronunciation of Cholmondeley as "Chumley" or the elision of St. Aldate's into "St. Oles." It is even better illustrated in this soccer limerick about a tall Oxford goalkeeper who lived in St. Aldate's:

There was a young man of St. Aldate's [Oles]
Who stood in the varsity galdates [goals]
   The high ones with care
   He dispatched through the air
While the low ones he let through in shaldates. [shoals]

41

In 1874 came the first Oxford–Cambridge match, won by Oxford 1–0. The two-handed throw-in was decreed in 1882. All this time a furious debate was raging within the Football Association between those who wanted to keep the sport purely amateur, a game for gentlemen, and the more practical-minded who argued in favor of play for pay. Six times between 1875 and 1883 a simon-pure team of Old Etonians reached the Football Association Cup Final, pinnacle of English soccer, and in 1882 defeated the Blackburn Rovers, a team of weavers and other craftsmen tainted with professionalism. When in 1883 the Rovers—again facing the Old Etonians—won, the end of the amateur in Football Association Cup competition loomed as inevitable.

In 1885 professionalism in soccer was legalized. In 1886 an international board was formed with two members each from the Football Associations of England, Scotland, Wales, and Ireland. In 1913 two were added from the Federation Internationale de Football Associations, and this ten-man body still makes the rules for soccer throughout the world.

Goal nets came in 1890 and the penalty kick in 1891. In 1901 England's first 100,000-plus soccer crowd watched as Tottenham Hotspur and Sheffield United tied 2–2 at the Crystal Palace in the Cup Final. Attendance: 110,802.

All this time soccer was spreading around the world. Its missionaries were British sailors who played the game for recreation when they were laid up in distant ports. The foreigners liked what they saw and took up the game. In 1904 the Federation Internationale de Football Associations was founded with France, Belgium, Switzerland, Holland, Denmark, Sweden, and Spain represented. Now one hundred and thirty nations belong to the worldwide federation. England ignored FIFA at the start—why should the mother country of the sport bow to foreign regulation—became affiliated in 1924, only to withdraw in 1928 when FIFA asserted its position with the International Olympic Committee as the supreme governing body of soccer.

Only after World War II did the British associations rejoin FIFA.

From the turn of the century on, English soccer clubs, in the well-known pattern of professionalism, tried to buy championships by buying up star players. In 1908 the Football Association attempted in vain to clamp the lid on wild spending for star players. It ordered that the maximum transfer (sales) fee would be £350 (about $850 in current exchange and perhaps $5,000 then). This stern edict was inspired by the payment of £1,000 in 1905 by Middlesborough to Sunderland for Alf Common.

But the restriction lasted only three months and since then transfer fees have climbed steadily. In 1957 Juventus paid £65,000 for John Charles of Leeds United and Wales, a wise investment because Juventus became Italian League champion in 1957–58. The record, however, is the £116,000 ($330,000 at the time) that Turin of Italy paid for Denis Law of Manchester United, and of this £40,000, or about $115,000, went to Law himself—a practice that American football and baseball players would like to see enforced on this side of the Atlantic, where none of the money involved in a purchase goes to the individual whose skill created his value.

One of the most important changes in the rules of soccer came in 1925 when it was decreed that a man was off side—barring certain technical and field position limitations—unless there were two opposing fullbacks between him and the goal. Formerly three opposing players were required. Billy McCracken, a Newcastle United fullback, is commonly regarded as the man directly responsible for the change. When an opposing team was pressing an attack, McCracken would run up the field a short distance, leaving only two teammates on defense. This would immediately make the attackers off side, calling for a kick. The stoppages in the game became exasperating.

Primarily the off-side change was made because attendance

43

at soccer matches had fallen off in England after the close of World War I, for the simple reason that too few goals were being scored. The rule makers hoped this innovation would liven up the game, just as later the National Professional Soccer League hoped its point-standings change would lead to more scoring. Results were not as expected. A mastermind of soccer, Herbert Chapman of Arsenal, who believed in tight defensive play, came up with the answer to the new rules for off-side. Chapman pulled the center halfback behind even the fullbacks and made him the ultimate defense in front of the goalkeeper. The center halfback became the policeman, the barrier, the bodyguard, the fence. The Swedes even called him the overcoat because of the way he hung onto the center forward, soccer's chief scorer. So soccer found itself again with the problem of how to restore the excitement of scoring.

In 1930 the wide international nature of the game was recognized by the establishment of the World Cup competition with an elaborate series of preliminary matches. The World Cup is contested every four years, in between the Olympic Games which decide the world amateur soccer championship.

Despite big transfer fees, soccer players in England and in most places around the world are poorly paid by American standards. There are, of course, spectacular exceptions such as Pelé, the idol of Brazil, whose earnings are in excess of $200,000 yearly. In Italy where big business concerns own the soccer teams and public interest is intense the salaries are substantial, but in England only about a dozen stars get into the $600 weekly bracket. The average pay is closer to $100 per week. Even taking into account the fact that the cost of living is substantially lower than in the United States and Canada, possibly by a half, the English player's salary is far from lavish.

Throughout most of its history soccer around the world has been unusually free of scandals, but in 1965 the biggest ever rocked the British national game. Ten players, including two stars of the English national team, were jailed and suspended for life for accepting bribes to lose league games. In addition to the ten jailed players, thirty-five others were named in a dossier drawn up by the police.

The two English stars involved in the scandal were center halfback Peter Swan and left halfback Tony Kay. The assize court found them guilty of conspiring to help Sheffield Wednesday lose an English first division game against Ipswich Town in 1962. Both were sentenced to four months in jail.

James Gauld, a former Mansfield Town player who blew the lid off the scandal by selling the story to a Sunday newspaper, got a four-year sentence.

When the scandal broke it appeared to be a crippling body blow to England's World Cup prospects. Swan and Kay both figured importantly in preparations for the World Cup of 1966. Surprisingly, England found substitutes and went on to win the World Cup. Swan and Kay were suspended from soccer for life by the Football Association.

The scandal was something new in the ninety-year course of English league soccer. True, there had been isolated cases of players accepting bribes and being suspended, but this was a widespread plot to fix games. Understandably, it created a sensation in a country where 12,000,000 people bet on the soccer pools every week. The fans waited to see what the next chapter in the uproar would be. However, the police took no further action after the initial arrests. Soccer went on as before, except that the convicted stars had disappeared from the scene.

The English league system has been copied by nearly every soccer nation of the world. There are four divisions in English soccer with twenty-two teams in both the first and second divisions, and twenty-four in both the third and fourth. The first division is top dog.

Each year the last two clubs in the first division are demoted to the second division, and the top two in the second move up to the first. The bottom two in the second drop to the third and the top two in the third are promoted; the bottom four in the third division are demoted and the top four in the fourth are elevated. Four independent clubs are then chosen to replace the bottom four that were demoted.

It is a system that might well be studied profitably by American sports, putting emphasis as it does not only on winning the league championship, but on staying out of the cellar as well.

6

Soccer's struggle to survive in the United States

———◆———

By one of those delicious ironies in human events, American college football is erecting a shrine and hall of fame at Rutgers University in New Brunswick, New Jersey, inspired by the fact that a game of soccer was played there November 6, 1869.

This puts football on a par with baseball, which built its Hall of Fame at Cooperstown, New York, and heaped laurels on General Abner Doubleday, despite the fact that the first modern baseball game was played on the Elysian Fields in Hoboken, New Jersey, and the good General was nowhere about at the time.

The excuse for the hall of fame at Rutgers is that the game played there later evolved into American football as the twentieth century came to know it, but football it most certainly was not in 1869.

The ball was round, it had to be kicked and not carried under the arm or thrown; to score it had to be propelled between two goalposts eight paces apart, and a goal counted only one point.

47

Considerable physical contact was permitted and there were twenty-five players to a team but otherwise the revered game in which Rutgers defeated Princeton 6–4 was soccer. As in soccer the field was almost square, 360 by 225 feet, and the players wore no protection. Two players on each team were stationed near the opposing team's goal (clearly off side by soccer's rules) in the hope of being able to retrieve a loose ball and kick it in for a point. That left twenty-three players on each team for action in midfield, with eleven of these serving as defenders and terming themselves fielders, and twelve making up the attack, and called bulldogs. It was agreed that when a total of ten goals was reached the game would end.

Yet college football, with not even a polite bow in the direction of soccer, cherishes the occasion as the fountainhead of a game that is now played with a pointed ball that is rarely kicked and where the hands have ascendancy over the feet.

Actually it was touch and go after the Civil War whether soccer would become the dominant American collegiate sport, or whether it would be Rugby which could expand into American football. In the end, Rugby-football won, thanks largely to the prestige of Harvard. Soccer it was that Princeton undergraduates played from 1820 on, calling it ballown, and soccer was what the two lower classes of Harvard played from 1827 until 1860, when the faculty put an end to it. The game took place on the first Monday of the college year; Yale played it in 1840, and Amherst and Brown knew it. Columbia put it on the intercollegiate level in 1870 and in the same year Cornell organized a soccer club. Yale resumed the game in 1872, modeling its rules on those of England's Football Association.

But while these colleges were going down the soccer road, one institution elected to play a different kind of game. In 1871 Harvard introduced what it called the "Boston game," patterned on Rugby and allowing players to run with the ball.

"Had it not been for the fact that Harvard's rules varied so much from those of the other colleges as to lead it to seek ·

games with a Canadian Rugby team, the pattern of the American game might never have changed from soccer," Allison Danzig asserts in *The History of American Football*.

Soccer was firmly in the saddle when representatives of Yale, Columbia, Princeton, and Rutgers met in the Fifth Avenue Hotel in New York on October 19, 1873, and formed the American Intercollegiate Football Association with rules modeled on the soccer rules of the London Football Association. Harvard would have no part of this.

The very next year McGill University of Montreal challenged Harvard to a football game that resembled Rugby. Harvard, shut out of intercollegiate soccer, accepted eagerly. The rules of play at the two schools varied slightly. The first game at Cambridge under Harvard's rules was won by the home team 3–0, and the second, also at Cambridge but under McGill's rules, ended in a scoreless tie. The third game at Montreal was won by Harvard 3–0.

Harvard took Rugby to its bosom and set out on a missionary campaign. Yale was challenged in 1875 and a game was played under "concessionary rules," meaning that Harvard agreed to certain changes favoring soccer and Yale conceded to play fifteen men. Running with the ball and tackling by gorilla embrace were permitted. Harvard not only won the game 4–0 but also won converts at Yale, and even at Princeton, which had sent observers. Princeton, after heated campus argument, voted in 1876 to adopt the Rugby game and invitations were sent to Harvard, Yale, and Columbia to meet in Springfield, Massachusetts. There the Intercollegiate Football Association adopted the modified Rugby Union code, soccer was banished from the prestigious top level of American education, and American-type football started its slow evolution.

Although it lost out in the academies, soccer in its pure form did continue to grow in both the United States and Canada, but with painful slowness. In 1888, Canada was able to send a team to England, and at about the same time in the eastern

49

United States, Scotch, Irish, and English immigrants were fostering soccer in New York, New Jersey, and New England. Then the game spread inconspicuously westward to St. Louis, Chicago, Detroit, Cincinnati, Cleveland, Denver, and San Francisco. Later German immigrants would play a major role in the sport.

In 1884 the American Football Association—for soccer—was founded in Newark, New Jersey, and in 1886 a game was played in Central Park in New York City.

In 1904 came the first invasion from overseas. The Pilgrims, a squad selected from British amateur teams, took on American teams. It was no contest. The Pilgrims won twenty-one games, lost only two. They were followed in 1906 by the Corinthian Football Club of London with much the same result: thirteen victories, one defeat, two ties. Both the Pilgrims and the Corinthians returned again with equally disastrous results for their American opponents.

In 1914 the United States formally entered the international soccer arena by forming the United States Football Association, which was recognized by FIFA. But like so many sports organizations designed to promote love of mankind and good sportsmanship, the FA was born in strife. There was a fierce struggle at first between the American Football Association, which controlled professional leagues in the Northeast, and the American Amateur Football Association. Each sought the blessing of FIFA. (It must be admitted that the word "professional" is used loosely here. Pay of $10 a game was considered good.)

FIFA sensibly told the two associations to compose their differences and come back as one unit. The inevitable wrangling began in 1912 and continued until the professionals withdrew from the talks. Meanwhile the amateurs had won powerful converts to their cause. Representatives of the strong eastern amateur clubs then joined in setting up the new organization, the United States Football Association, and FIFA recognized it as the governing body of soccer in the United States. The professional American Football Association promptly acted on the adage, If you can't lick 'em, join 'em, and voted to come in under the USFA umbrella. From 1914 on this is the organization that has controlled both amateur soccer and professional soccer in the United States, the only change being to insert soccer into the name in deference to the national feeling that football is something not played with the feet.

It cannot help but be observed that rancorous struggles between governing bodies in sports in the United States seem to be rooted in the national character; the National Football League vs. the American Football League and its predecessor; the American Amateur Athletic Union vs. the National Collegiate Athletic Association; and even in its early days the National Baseball League versus the upstart American Baseball League.

In Canada the Dominion Football Association was founded in 1873, and the present ruling body, the Canadian Football Association, recognized by FIFA, was incorporated in 1923 somehow with considerably less table-pounding than went on south of the border.

Although soccer was far from popular in the United States in the Roaring Twenties, curiously enough a team was put together from professional ranks that finished third in the first World Cup competition ever held, that in 1930 in Montevideo. True, only four European teams entered the tournament (England was conspicuously absent) and the United States team included six naturalized English professionals. Nevertheless the United States team impressed observers as exceptionally big and strong and it was given the honor of heading up one of the four pools. It fully justified its selection, defeating Belgium 3–0 in its first game. Paraguay, the South American champion and favorite in the pool, was toppled by the same score in the second game. Marcel Pinel, one of the players on the French team, described the Americans this way:

"We called them the 'weight-putters.' They always amused

51

us when we saw them training, for they were always clad in tiny shorts which revealed enormous thighs, like tree trunks, and they would go lapping and slogging round and round the track like long distance runners. They were certainly on the crude side."

The crude Americans played with three forwards up front and the rest of the team massed before the nets. In their games against Belgium and Paraguay they scored two first-half goals and then wore down the opposition.

The victory in its pool advanced the United States to the semifinals where it took the field as the favorite against Argentina only to lose rather humiliatingly 6–0, but not before contributing one of the more enduring anecdotes in soccer's annals. The referee, John Langenus, called a foul against an American in some furious goal action. This brought the American trainer running onto the field carrying, for no particular reason, his medical kit. After addressing himself vehemently to Langenus he threw down the kit in a burst of temper. The case broke, bottles were shattered, and a heavy odor of chloroform enveloped both referee and belligerent trainer. It served to calm all concerned.

Although the United States won third place in this first of all World Cups, the good showing failed to stimulate intense interest in the sport back home. Soccer barely stumbled along in the country, falling to such a low point that when in 1941 the executive secretary of the United States Soccer Football Association died suddenly, Joe J. Barriskill, a soccer buff who had emigrated from Ireland when he was eighteen, gave up business and ran the USSFA for two years out of his own pocket. He was still on the job a quarter-century later. Happily by this time he was also on the payroll.

The high-water mark of American soccer was reached June 27, 1950, when an American team, recruited from among the best players of St. Louis, Chicago, New York, Philadelphia, Fall River, Massachusetts, and Pittsburgh, to the vast astonishment of the soccer world, defeated England in the World Cup preliminaries at Belo Horizonte, Brazil, by a score of 1–0. America's third place in 1930 was scored against lesser breeds without the law; England was the mother country of the sport, the very touchstone of its tradition. Furthermore this was England's first appearance in World Cup competition and the team comprised the best players in every position that English professional soccer could provide. Speculation before the momentous game with the United States centered only on whether England could defeat Brazil, the up and coming Latin-American power. The English team included in its ranks Stanley Matthews, then the greatest soccer player in the world, but for strange and mysterious reasons he sat on the sidelines.

The English players took the field laughing and confident. They made no attempt to score a quick goal and, in fact, allowed the Yankees time to collect themselves and start playing as a team. The Brazilian crowd soon showed its partiality by cheering the Americans' every good play.

The lone, all-important goal came five minutes before the half. A well-placed kick from the right wing sent the ball to the center of the field. Joseph Gaetjens jumped, slammed his forehead into it and the ball whistled into the nets.

Still it seemed only a question of time before the star-studded English team would settle down and make short work of the upstarts. But the Americans, rallied by Frank Borghi and John and Ed Souza, played an inspired defensive game and as victors were deservedly carried off the field by the excited crowd.

The depth of the tragedy was described afterwards by Stanley Matthews:

"I sat with bowed head until the players left the field. I never thought I would live to see this. As I raised my head to look around me I felt a pain in most of my fingers. I looked down at my hands and saw spots of blood on the palms. I had been so

tense in the closing minutes of the match I had dug my finger-
nails into my flesh without at the time feeling a thing."

He went to the English dressing room and found a climate
that caused him to comment, "I wouldn't like to describe what
I met there so I will draw a veil over it."

While Dunkirk and Tobruk were merely setbacks that illu-
minated the final victory in World War II, Belo Horizonte
seemed the bottom of an abyss for England. England also lost
to Spain in a rough game, and the eventual winner of the Cup
was not Brazil, but Uruguay. The United States lost its other
preliminary rounds in the Cup matches, to Spain 3–1, and to
Chile 5–2, both good games. Even before the World Cup upset
of England, there was proof that soccer skill was on the rise
on this side of the Atlantic when the Kearny–Philadelphia
eleven tied Manchester United, a first division English team,
2–2 in the spring of 1950.

Soccer enthusiasm in the United States dipped again after
that memorable game in Brazil. Yet with more and more top
European and Latin-American teams coming to the United States
for exhibition matches that educated crowds in the fine points
of the game, the way was paved for Bill Cox to launch his short-
lived International Soccer League in 1960.

Another pioneer soccer promoter on the scene was Enzo
Magnozzi, a former real estate operator and longtime aficionado
of the game. Magnozzi was responsible for both of Pelé's appearances at Yankee Stadium in 1966 and 1967 as well as the
staging of exhibitions between other foreign teams. The 1966
Yankee Stadium crowd paid $232,000 at the gate, highest ever
for a soccer exhibition game in North America. Of the receipts
five percent went the United States Soccer Football Association for permission to stage the match and the expenses and
fees to the two teams exceeded eighty percent. In 1967 Magnozzi, with a total gate despite rain of $170,000, paid the usual
five percent to the USSFA but in addition had to promise ten
percent, or $17,000, to Madison Square Garden, whose Skyliners

Players battle for possession of the ball. Players here on the left seem on the verge of dancing. Man in shirt with the number 35 seems intent on disrupting the embrace. Number 60 races to the scene to aid his teammates.

Soccer is played in stadiums of various sizes and shapes. The Maracoma Stadium in Rio de Janeiro, Brazil, which has held more than 200,000 for a big soccer game, is the biggest of them all. The protective moat around the playing field is clearly visible.

Although soccer originated in England, Russian crowds have taken it to their bosoms. Here is the great Central Lenin Stadium in Moscow which is almost always filled to its 103,000 capacity for big soccer games. (In this photograph the stadium is being used for a mass meeting honoring Fidel Castro.)

Sir Stanley Matthews, England's and possibly the world's most durable sportsman, is the first and only soccer player ever knighted by the queen. Here Matthews is seen still agile and fast in the twilight of an astounding thirty-year career.

Pelé, in light uniform, considered the world's greatest soccer player, in action with the Santos team from São Paulo, Brazil, attracted a capacity crowd at Randall's Island, New York, in 1966.

A typically American touch in soccer was the introduction of pretty cheerleaders. Here the girls whip up enthusiasm for the hometown Baltimore Bays in their contest with the Oakland Clippers for the National Professional Soccer League championship.

Guy St. Vil of the Baltimore Bays charges in to get possession of the ball as a teammate, Leif Klasson, protects his head. This fast action occurred in the National Professional Soccer League's first championship game in Baltimore, September 3, 1967. Baltimore beat the Oakland Clippers by a 1–0 score. Oakland took the second game in Oakland 4–1 and clinched the title on the aggregate score.

The ruling triumvirate of soccer in the United States. From left to right, Ken Macker, president of the Western Conference of the North American Soccer League; John Anderson of the Detroit Cougars, chairman of the league's executive committee, and Dick Walsh, president of the Eastern Conference.

in the United Soccer Association had been granted New York City exclusivity by the USSFA (an exclusivity that the National Professional Soccer League's New York Generals defied).

Magnozzi bid for a team franchise when professional soccer started in earnest in 1967, but like Bill Cox he found no takers for his talents.

It can be seen from all this that considerable promotional activity preceded the launching of professional soccer in 1967, and strong evidence had been produced that there was money to be had on the soccer pitch.

Long before the burst of soccer interest in the 1960's, soccer existed on an organized albeit obscure basis in the United States. Ever since the 1912–13 season there has been a National Challenge Cup—donated by Sir Thomas R. Dewar, a British sportsman—which goes to the top American professional team after a series of eliminations leading up to the Cup Final. Starting with the 1922–23 season there has also been a National Amateur Challenge Cup.

Although far from the national level, a new trophy of peculiarly deep sentimental value was added to the growing cluster of soccer awards in 1967. Weston David MacLean of Westbury, Long Island, was a goalie of great promise who loved the game with all his heart. A lance corporal in the United States Marine Corps, he died in action outside Da Nang on July 22, 1966, a few days after his nineteenth birthday. MacLean had turned down a college scholarship to enlist in the Marines. Before he went overseas he left a letter with his mother to be opened only in the event of his death. In it he instructed that his savings of $400 be turned over to the Long Island Junior Soccer League. The League instituted the Wes MacLean trophy to be given each year to a high school goalie on Long Island.

The American Soccer League was founded in 1933 and with the National League, the German-American League, and the Continental League in Los Angeles constituted soccer's top level in the nation prior to Cox's International Soccer League and the advent of the National Professional Soccer League and the United Soccer Association.

Before the NPSL and the USA came on the scene, American soccer professionals were not exactly overpaid. Most received around $20 for a game, and some as high as $60. Crowds of 1,000 were considered satisfactory and 3,000 rather sensational. The Challenge Cup Finals sometimes drew up to 5,000.

But there had been a steady growth in interest in the game, paving the way for the NPSL and the USA. By the time these two appeared, the United States Soccer Football Association had 25,000 amateurs registered on its lists, 1,500 professionals, plus 10,000 juniors not connected with high schools or colleges. Whereas a quarter-century earlier the state of California had twenty teams it now had more than four hundred. More than two hundred colleges were in the Intercollegiate Soccer Football Association and ever since 1958 the National Collegiate Athletic Association had conducted a full-scale championship.

Brian Glanville, the eminent soccer columnist of the *Sunday Times* of London, spent the summer of 1967 in the United States and went away with mixed feelings of hope for the future and difficulties in the present.

The visit, he wrote in the *F. A. News*, official publication of the English Football Association, "left me with an impression of the glorious possibilities and the dire problems faced by soccer in America. Perhaps the direst of all is that the game remains in essence an un-American activity, the kind which might usefully have been investigated by the late Senator Joe McCarthy. If, in the course of the past half century, soccer has obstinately remained a very minor American sport, if it is necessary, now, to introduce it, as they were saying over there, 'from the top,' for millionaires to pour in a Niagara of money, it has plainly been for good and profound reasons."

Mr. Glanville felt that "the Americans (in the past) rejected soccer because it didn't speak to them, because in some strange way, it didn't interlock with the national character; if you like, the national unconscious. The American kind of football, on the other hand, and baseball, did . . .

"American football . . . is enormously violent, highly complicated and episodic. Soccer, by contrast, despite an ominous trend towards negative play, remains fluid, improvisational and continuous."

Nevertheless, the backers of the National Professional Soccer League and the United Soccer Association felt—and still feel—strongly that as soccer built up at the adolescent level, as teams achieved definite city identification, as stars and personalities emerged, as television continued to spread its message of a fast and exciting game, the national conscious and unconscious would accept the game for what it is—the world's best.

7

*How to enjoy the game; the
rules explained*

———◆———

The best way to enjoy soccer is to sit back and relax. This is advice, however, rarely followed around the world. Far from being relaxed, many, if not most soccer fans are enthusiastic, vocal, vehement—even violent. In Latin-American countries it is common to separate the playing field from the stands with a moat and a wire fence to prevent attacks on players and particularly on the referee.

The Teams

Soccer is truly the simplest of all sports. Eleven men wearing uniforms of one color try to propel a harlequin-hued ball about the size of a basketball past eleven men wearing uniforms of another color into a large netted goal, using only their feet and their heads. The heads can be used two ways: cerebrally, to outthink opponents, and physically, to advance the ball by butting and bouncing it—a tactic not recommended for migraine sufferers. The hands may never be used except by the goalkeeper. (As it is important to distinguish the goalkeeper clearly, he wears a uniform of a different color than his teammates.) A goal counts as one point. That's all there is to it.

The Uniforms

A soccer player's equipment is also extremely simple. He wears a jersey and shorts but none of the padding of football. No helmets are worn and regulation shoes are soft and low-cut, much like a distance runner's. The shoes may have bars or cleats but a player is forbidden to wear anything that might be dangerous to another player. If bars are used they are made of leather or rubber. Studs may be of leather, rubber, aluminum, plastic or similar material but they must be at least a half-inch in diameter. Neither bars nor studs may be more than three quarters of an inch long. Protruding nails are forbidden. Thus soccer cleats are much less dangerous than the sharp metal bars of baseball; they more resemble those on American football shoes. A player may wear shin guards under his long socks, for most soccer injuries center on the ankles and legs. The inexpensiveness of soccer equipment, along with the simplicity of the game, has brought it into increasing popularity in North American secondary schools and colleges.

The Field

Because soccer was born in England, and because the English attitude toward certain formalities is delightfully casual, the size of a soccer field, or *pitch* as it is called in the land of its origin, is amazingly elastic. The field can be as long as 130 yards or as short as 100, as wide as 100 or as narrow as 50.

But as soccer has spread around the world, a field 115 yards long and 75 yards wide has gained acceptance as being the most desirable. The ball has been standardized as being 27 to

28 inches in diameter. At each end of the field are the goals, eight yards wide and eight feet high, with netting sloping from the top crossbar to the ground outside the playing field. In each corner of the field a flag on a flexible pole is placed. Half the length of the field a line is drawn which in American football would be the fifty-yard line. In the center of this is a circle with a 10-yard radius. Play starts in this circle at the beginning of the game, at the second half and after each goal. A coin is tossed and the winning team may either kick off or select the goal it wishes to defend. Both teams must be in their own half of the field when play starts. The circle with the 10-yard radius underlines a fundamental rule of soccer. Players on the opposing side must be ten yards from the ball on the kickoff, or after a free kick, goal kick, or corner kick. Corner kicks, to be explained later, are made from a pie-shaped marking with a one-yard radius at each of the four corners. (*Diagram follows this chapter.*)

Length of Game

Like American football, soccer is divided into halves, but unlike American football there are no time-outs except for serious injuries or the time needed to put the ball back into play when it goes outside the playing field. Each half consists of forty-five minutes of furious action. Soccer is a game for finely trained distance runners with the ability to sprint with the best, and capable of sustaining the pummeling of hard physical contact.

The Goal

At each end of the soccer field, surrounding the goal and its net, is what is known as the penalty area, a space 44 yards by 18. Infractions of the rules within this area can be almost fatal to the defending team, particularly when it is considered that many soccer games are decided by a single goal. If the referee calls a major foul in the area, a penalty kick is awarded the offensive team. Only the goalkeeper is between the kicker, who stands on a marked spot twelve yards out, and the enormous goal net. In this circumstance a score is almost automatic because soccer kickers are that adept.

The penalty area is also the place where the goalkeeper can touch the ball with his hands without being penalized. Inside the penalty area, directly in front of the nets, is the goal area, six yards by twenty yards. When a goal kick is being taken— that is, the ball is being put into play by the defending team after having gone over the goal line (but not into the nets), having been touched last by an offensive player—it must be kicked from this area. If the goalkeeper has possession of the ball, or is obstructing an opponent, he may be charged inside this area.

When a goalkeeper grabs the ball and prevents a score he can take the ball out to the edge of the penalty area and then boot it downfield to put his team on the offensive. For many years goalies were allowed to bounce the ball three times, taking four steps between each bounce, as they maneuvered to the edge of the goal area. This is called bouncing in soccer, not dribbling as in basketball. Dribbling in soccer means controlling the ball with the feet. FIFA threw a sneaky curve at hard-beset goalkeepers in 1967 when it ruled that they could not take more than four steps in all with the ball. Finally this restriction was clarified to give goalkeepers permission to dribble the ball with their feet as well as take four steps with it and bounce it three times. The rule was designed to prevent time-wasting by goalkeepers, most of whom reacted angrily.

"What am I expected to do if I can't reach a teammate after taking four steps—swallow the ball?" fumed Gordon Banks, England's goalkeeper in the 1966 World Cup victory.

Because, even with the new restricting rule, goalkeepers can maneuver more readily with the ball, it is a common sight in soccer to see a goalkeeper, after a goal kick has been awarded, kick the ball gently outside the penalty area to a teammate who then returns it to him. Taking advantage of this maneuver the goalie can now advance to the edge of the penalty area for a mighty kick downfield.

Advancing the Ball

There are three methods that can be used to bring the ball downfield to a position where it can be maneuvered into the nets of the goal:

One is by either long or short kicks.

Another is by dribbling, in which a player advances the ball with loving little taps as he runs along practically on top of it.

The third is by heading, in which the forehead is used as a bat.

Out of Bounds

Inevitably soccer balls are accidentally kicked outside the playing area. They are put back in play in a variety of ways. If the ball is kicked over the sideline (or *touchline,* to give it its proper name) the ball is given to a player on the team opposed to the one that touched it last. He must stand with both feet on the ground and both hands on the ball, which he throws back into play from over his head.

If the ball goes over the line at the end of the field where the goal is located, entirely different methods come into play.

If the attacking team propelled it over the goal line, the ball is placed in the goal area, which is the twenty- by six-yard box directly in front of the nets. It is then usually kicked out very vigorously by the goalkeeper, or if his foot happens to be a bit sore or inaccurate, by one of his teammates. Or as explained previously, he may kick it barely outside the penalty area—providing the opposing team is well away from the goal —to a teammate who returns it to him. He can then advance to the very edge of the penalty area for his kick downfield, and take advantage of an additional twelve yards. During the course of the game, again assuming there are no dangerous opponents nearby, a player may kick or butt the ball to the goalkeeper to get advantage of a booming kick from the limit of the penalty area. All of these maneuvers are on the risky side. If the ball eludes the goalkeeper during any one of them, it can easily go into the net and score a goal for the other team.

If the defending team propelled the ball over the goal line it is placed in the one-yard arc at either corner of the field at the defensive end. This is a corner kick. A good curve-ball kicker can even score on such a kick, but more commonly the ball is lofted to a teammate near the mouth of the goal who then tries to butt or kick it in.

The Officials

Control of a soccer game is vested in one man, the referee, as compared to the flock of officials who cover the landscape in baseball and football. There are two linesmen to assist the referee but their responsibilities are limited. They indicate by waving their little flags when the ball has crossed the goal line or the sideline and they designate which team is entitled to possession of the ball. They may assist in off-side decisions but in all vital matters it is the referee alone who makes the decisions.

The Nine Deadly Sins

There are nine things a soccer player must never, never do: he must not hold an opponent; he must not strike or attempt to strike an opponent (a wide-open area of dispute, it must be admitted); nor push an opponent; nor handle the ball (excepting the goalkeeper); he must not kick or attempt to kick an opponent (and in a game where the footwork is fast and furious what constitutes an attempted kick would test the wisdom of Solomon); nor jump at an opponent; nor trip an

63

opponent; or charge in a dangerous manner; nor charge an opponent from behind unless he is intentionally obstructed.

The kick that is awarded to the opposite team for these nine serious infractions of the rules is a direct free kick. That is, a goal can be scored from it. If any of these offenses occur outside the penalty area, the defending team can line up a wall of players at a distance of ten yards from the ball, usually four or five men in all with locked arms, to guard against a goal, assuming the kick is close enough to raise that threat.

Minor Infractions

There are also minor technical offenses which result in indirect free kicks, from which a goal cannot be scored until the ball has been played by any two players.

These minor infractions are: intentionally obstructing an opponent without trying to play the ball; being off side (which will be explained later); breaking the rules persistently; disagreeing too vehemently with the referee's decision; conduct that is ungentlemanly (and as there is no Social Register to consult, only the referee can decide when a player ceases to be a gentleman); kicking the ball a second time after making a kickoff, throw-in, corner kick, or goal kick before anyone else has had a chance at it; and violation of the bouncing rule by the goalkeeper.

As in the case of the much more serious penalty kick, opposing players must be ten yards from the kicker on a direct free kick.

Off-side

To the newcomer to soccer the off-side penalty is the most puzzling of all, and often the most difficult to see. The rule is that at all times there must be two opponents between an attacker and the defense's goal, one of whom of course is usually the goalkeeper. The idea is to prevent an attacking team from stationing a good kicker close to the goal and then getting off a lucky pass to him. But a player is not off side if he is in his own half of the field, or the ball was last touched by an opponent, or he is behind the ball when it is played to him, or —and here is that all-seeing, all-knowing, referee again—he wasn't intentionally off side.

The Ball in Play

In soccer a ball is in play until it has completely crossed over the sideline or the goal line or into the nets for a score. As long long as any part of it is in the playing field it is in action. Furthermore, a goal is scored even if the ball is caught by the goalkeeper inside the net, providing the ball has completely passed through the goal bars.

When a ball crosses over the sideline or touchline, it is put back into play by the opposing team of the player who touched it last. This is done by a throw-in. The thrower must have both feet on the ground and both hands on the ball and must throw from over his head.

The Art of Kicking

Since kicking looms so large in soccer, it is interesting to note that while sometimes the toe or instep is used as in American football, more commonly the inside of the foot or even the outside is employed to make a short pass to a teammate. Use of the inside of the foot has an awkward look; the player must position one foot alongside the ball, usually on the run, and raise the other leg sideways and backwards for a swinging clout at the ball. But the end result is accuracy and distance exceeding the best kickers in football, and with the great stars of the game, super-speed as well. The accuracy comes from the fact that a much greater expanse of shoe leather is applied to the ball than can be obtained with the toe or instep.

In fact, the accuracy of the common soccer kick has come to be widely respected in American football. Each year more kickers use the soccer style, particularly for field goals. The Gogolak brothers, Peter and Charlie, led the way in professional football. They came from college ranks, but possibly the most astounding of the soccer kickers was Garo Ypremian, an Armenian born on Cyprus, who was only an indifferent soccer player. He walked into a practice session of the Detroit Lions and gave such an impressive kicking demonstration that he was signed on the spot despite the fact he stood only five-foot-five and weighed 150, average soccer dimensions. In 1966 against the Minnesota Vikings he kicked six field goals of 33, 26, 15, 20, 28, and 33 yards for eighteen points and a new professional record. The soccer-style kick is a welcome guest in American football.

In 1966 the University of California at Los Angeles football team acquired Zenon Andrusyshyn from the track team. He was a Canadian of Ukrainian descent with a soccer background. He has to his credit a 65-yard field goal in practice, and under fire has scored often from forty yards. In 1966 with success in seventeen out of nineteen conversions and eight out of sixteen field goals attempted he was ninth in the nation in total scoring —all done soccer-style.

Drop Ball

A rare situation is the drop ball. This happens when a ball is locked between two opposing players and the referee stops play. Action is resumed when the referee drops the ball between a player from each team.

Substitutes

In World Cup play substitutes are forbidden. If a man is seriously injured his team goes on playing without him. Since

1966 substitutes have become generally accepted in a limited number. Professional soccer in the United States permits three substitutes: the goalie and two players. Pressure is mounting in the rest of the world for liberalization of the no-substitute rule.

True Football

Probably the most vivid impression a newcomer gets at a soccer game is that it is really and truly football, except for those dramatic moments when it becomes headball. The ball is in almost constant contact with the feet of the players. And those feet can do amazing, almost unbelievable things.

A good player can maneuver a ball through a group of opponents with side steps and dance movements as intricate as ballet. He can get under a ball that has been kicked high in the air and leaping up, can reverse its flight with his body well off the ground. He can even kick it over his head in the direction of the goal while stretched out flat in midair, not caring how hard he must fall to the ground afterwards. Or he can use his head as effectively and vigorously as his feet, the center of his forehead being the point of impact. Naturally, this is called "heading."

Heading

Heading developed slowly in soccer. There is nothing in the rules that prevents bouncing the ball off any part of the body, except of course the hands, but in the early days the advantage of using the head was not realized. It probably started accidentally. It has now been developed to a high degree of skill.

Some players find this technique painful and are reluctant to use it. Experts say, however, that once beginners learn how to strike the ball with the flat part of the forehead, where the skull is strongest, heading can be a decisive factor in the game.

It can be done from a stationary position, on the run, or while jumping, and the ball can be directed forward, sideways, or backward.

Soccer's Histrionics

Since so many soccer decisions rest on what a philosopher would call the subjective opinion of the referee, a high degree of drama is associated with the game. You could even call it hamming. If a player is trying to convince the referee that he has been fouled, particularly by being kicked, shoved, or tripped, what better way to do so than to fall to the ground and writhe in absolute agony. Of course if the referee is not interested in that particular bit of acting, and it is suddenly apparent that the aggrieved player is needed elsewhere on the field, he springs to his feet with astonishing vigor.

That is not to say that players are not injured in soccer. In such cases it is usually apparent to the referee and other contestants that something is wrong and play is stopped. Opponents can be as solicitous of an injured player as his own teammates. A trainer is sent out from the bench. But by the nature of the rules play must quickly be resumed, and if the injury is serious the player is taken off the field, with a substitute coming in if that is permissible. If substitutions are forbidden his team continues playing one man light until such time as he regains his strength.

Goalkeepers in particular have developed a highly histrionic touch. Most kicks from any distance are comparatively easy to judge but the leaps and catches that stop them can be highly theatrical. But there are saves that are genuinely spectacular.

Tackling, Dribbling, and Passing

Three common words in soccer immediately baffle American spectators. None means what an American thinks it does based on his knowledge of other sports.

68

Tackling here has nothing to do with the embrace that throws a mammoth football player to the ground. Dribbling has nothing to do with the deft bouncing of a basketball. Passing does not mean throwing the ball through the air.

Tackling means getting the ball away from an opponent by clever use of the feet. The defender jams his foot in the path of the ball, hopefully gains possession and goes his merry way. It is illegal to slide and trip the man in possession of the ball. But even a highly legal tackle can result in violent body contact.

Dribbling means controlling and moving the ball with the feet while running down the field. It is almost a mincing dance step but when a wiry soccer player dribbles a ball around or through the defenses of his opponents any impression that dribbling is effeminate disappears.

Passing means diverting the ball to a teammate, usually by a short kick close to the ground but sometimes by a long boot downfield.

Player Duties

Although the functions and duties of soccer players aside from the goalkeeper seem indeterminate and confused, actually there are clear-cut and sharply defined responsibilities.

If you will visualize the line drawn through the middle of the field and the ten-yard circle in the center of it, the man who stands in the very center of the circle at the kickoff is the center forward. He is usually the team's best scorer. To his immediate left is the inside left and near the left sideline of the field is the outside left. Similarly to his right is the inside right and near the right sideline the outside right. These five make up the forward wall, in classic soccer considered to be the purely offensive part of the team.

Some twenty yards back at kickoff are the left halfback and the right halfback. They are play makers, good dribblers, the men who set up a score. Parallel to them but directly in front of the goalkeeper is the center half, obviously a key defensive

69

player. At either side or in front of the penalty zone are the left fullback and the right fullback, also chiefly defensive.

That is the way many teams line up at the kickoff, which is not a kickoff at all in the American football sense. The center forward puts the ball in play with a short kick to a teammate and from that point on, no one, except the goalkeeper, remains in his starting position. As the game has evolved, strategists have changed their ideas about the forward wall and how it should go about scoring a goal. Different nations and different areas have created different styles. In England and in much of Europe, soccer has become more and more defensive. Games less and less were played for the enjoyment of spectators. Teams were satisfied to come away with a tie.

While Europe became more defense-minded, more rigidly automatic in its style of play, Latin America became more offense-bent, more individualistic.

South American players like to dribble, always a spectacular movement, and then divert the ball with a short kick to a nearby teammate. Europeans tend to run more and try for the long kicks.

After the close of World War II, soccer became almost letter-perfect in England and Europe. Scores were low, risky plays were few, serious penalties infrequent. But in South America the game became more dramatic, more personal, and often erupted into violence both on the field and in the stands.

Strategy and Tactics

One hears a lot of talk about strategy and tactics in soccer but formations as such do not mean much and even the names given the positions no longer carry the same responsibilities as of old.

Consider the famous W–M formation, now regarded as utterly old-fashioned.

Look at the diagram of a soccer field at the end of this chapter and imagine the left halfback and the right halfback have both dropped back and the inside left and the inside right have taken up positions on an imaginary line leading from the center halfback to the outside left and the outside right, you will have eight players in a formation that looks like a combination of a W (the five forwardmost players) and an M (the five nearest the goal, with of course the inside left and the inside right figuring in both letters). This, in theory, is the way British teams formerly deployed.

Most soccer technicians now think in terms of 4-2-4 or 4-3-3.

The first combination simply means that four men constitute the last line of defense in front of the goalkeeper; two carry the burden of controlling and advancing the ball in midfield and four are primarily offensive attackers. In 4-3-3 there are still four men in the last-ditch defensive assignments but one of the forward wall has joined the midfield squad.

Ron Greenwood, manager of England's famous West Ham team, does not think much of finespun theories or intricate deployments in soccer. He once told a coaching school, "Tactics is the last thing on the list. You get basic skills, you get fitness, you get intelligence, people thinking all the time. Football is imagination. When you've got these things the tactics take care of themselves."

So designations such as W–M, 4-2-4, or 4-3-3 are merely a means to tell players before the start of the game what their primary responsibilities will be. But if the opportunity presents itself even the fullbacks, the last line of defense, may charge down the field on attack.

Defensive Containment

Modern soccer aims first of all to contain, that is to say, to beat back the attack, and then to get possession of the ball and launch a counterattack.

71

Among the defenses aimed at containment two have gained popular names. They are both quite simple in theory. One is the "Swiss Bolt," in which nine men on the team (the goalkeeper, of course, must hold his position at the mouth of the goal) create a kind of defensive net outside of which a tenth man floats around hoping to catch an opponent unawares, get the ball, and summon his teammates to cooperate in scoring a goal. The Italians originated another type of the same Maginot Line tactic, called *Catenaccio*, except in their strategy the spare man operates behind the line, trying to make trouble if the opposing team should break through.

But usually a team is deployed chiefly with the intent of "marking" certain opponents. Marking means shadowing a man, in the hope of getting the ball away from him if and when he gets it and, certainly, to stay between him and the goal.

Fundamentally, the best strategy is one that makes it easier to get the ball into the goal net and thereby gain a point. As for the rules be assured that the referee sees all, knows all, and rules with an iron hand.

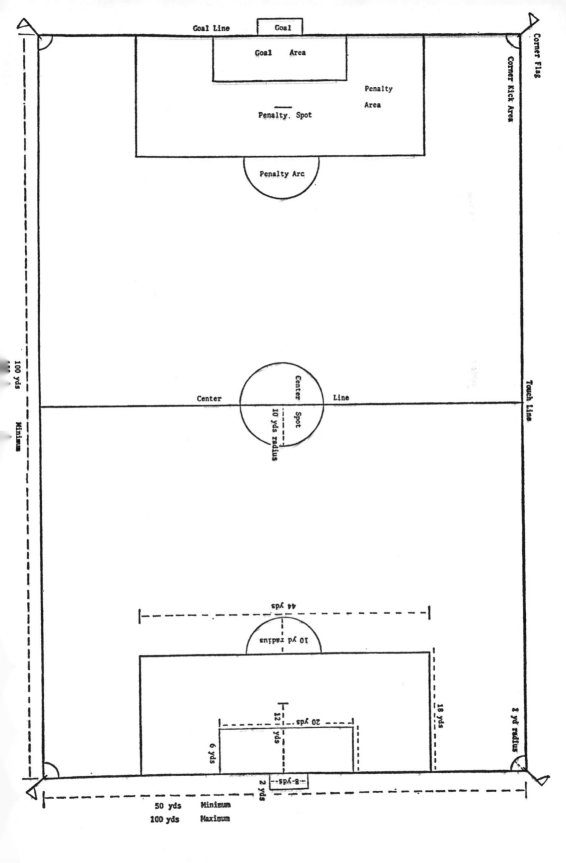

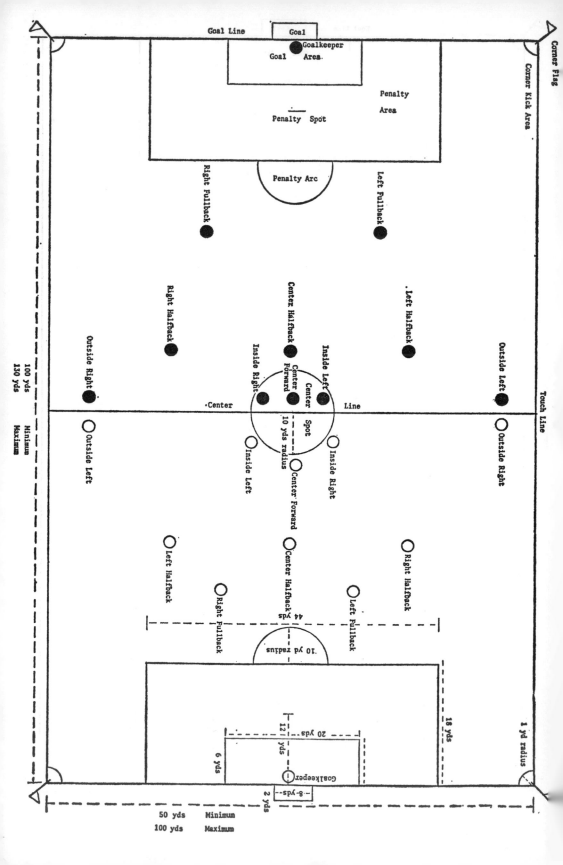

8

The all-powerful referee

———◆———

In the purest sense soccer does not have rules. It has Laws. Around the world the word is capitalized. The enforcer of these Laws, seventeen in number, is the referee, without question the most powerful official in the world of sports. In England when he enters the grounds for a game he is in absolute control not only of the players but also of the police, hired by the home soccer club. He is the sole judge of whether or not a game should be played if the weather is inclement or the field is in a dangerous condition. So absolute are his powers he can even send a player off the playing field before the game has started.

His power is epitomized by the penalty kick. This is awarded for any breach of the Laws restraining violence, and if the offense occurs within the penalty area with no one between the kicker and the goalkeeper it is almost an automatic score.

The referee in soccer is supposed to be gifted in mind reading, extrasensory perception and blind intuition because the Laws specifically command him to take into account the intentions as well as the actions of players. He can even ignore an infraction if he judges there was no intent to take advantage of an opponent or if the player who was fouled retains possession of the ball, in which case a penalty might work to the disadvantage of the offensive team. Everything depends on split-second, highly subjective decisions.

Here is the specific Law on fouls and misconduct:

"A player who intentionally commits any of the following nine offenses—

"(a) Kicks or attempts to kick an opponent;

"(b) Trips an opponent, i.e., throwing or attempting to throw him by use of the legs or by stopping in front or behind him;

"(c) Jumps at an opponent;

"(d) Charges an opponent in a violent or dangerous manner;

"(e) Charges an opponent from behind unless the latter be obstructing;

"(f) Strikes or attempts to strike an opponent;

"(g) Holds an opponent with his hand or any part of the arm;

"(h) Pushes an opponent with his hand or any part of the arm;

"(i) Handles the ball, i.e., carries, strikes, or propels the ball with his hand or arm (this does not apply to the goal keeper within his own penalty area);

"Shall be penalized by the award of a direct free kick to be taken by the opposing side from the place where the penalty occurred.

"Should a player of the defending side intentionally commit one of the above nine offenses within the penalty area he shall be penalized by a penalty kick.

"A penalty kick can be awarded irrespective of the position of the ball, if in play, at the time an offense within the penalty area is committed."

Note the words and phrases wide open to personal interpre-

74

tation: "intentionally commits ... attempting to throw ... violent or dangerous ... attempts to strike. ..."

Surely the man called on to run six to eight miles during the course of an hour and a half of play and at the same time render decisions based on hairline distinctions should be among the best-paid of sports officials, revered by his associates, and held in awe by spectators. Alas, around the world he is but a part-time employee, poorly paid, with no pension to look forward to, and all too often the target of violence.

And most amazing of all, there is no known case of corruption of a soccer referee, although due to the low-scoring nature of the game it would be easier for one to fix a match than it would for any other kind of sports official. The British even argue that paying referees more money would not make them any better; the fact that officiating is only a hobby with them serves to make them more courageous. In fact, the attitude of everyone intimately connected with soccer is that corruption of a referee is absolutely unthinkable. Yet all a referee receives for presiding over a match in any of the four top leagues in England is ten guineas and expenses. A guinea is a hoity-toity form of payment and means a pound plus a shilling. Ten guineas is about $25.

In America, the National Professional Soccer League, believing in the importance of solid English refereeing, imported its officials for the first season, budgeting each at $15,000–$16,000 including salary, travel expenses, and an allowance for the family. The United Soccer Association used American referees, paying them $40 and expenses per game.

American football officials are part-time employees, too, but by contrast National Football League referees get $300 and expenses for each game and $750 for the championship contest.

In Organized Baseball, umpires are on a yearly salary ranging from a minimum of $8,000 up to $20,000. On mandatory retirement at the age of fifty-seven, American League umpires get a pension of $5,100 per year; National League umpires fare better, with retirement not required until age sixty-five, and an annual pension of $7,800.

As one British referee said, "A player is in the game of soccer for what he can get out of it. A referee is in the game for the love of it." Other English referees in the National Professional Soccer League have summed up their job as follows:

Ken Stokes—"The Laws of the game can only be run by one man. A referee makes mistakes but as long as they are honest mistakes there is nothing to worry about. In fact, they should balance out over ninety minutes. The man who makes the fewest mistakes is the better referee."

Walter Crossley—"Refereeing is 10 percent knowledge of the Laws and 90 percent common sense."

Eddie Pearson—"And that 90 percent includes a lot of psychology."

How does a referee go about his Olympian task? Despite the fluid nature of the game, the referee uses a fixed pattern. Depending on the sun and the wind he selects an imaginary diagonal line running from one corner of the field to the opposite corner and stays fairly close to it. An opposite imaginary diagonal is drawn for the two linesmen and one of them is stationed along the side or touchline from midfield to the goal line and the other patrols the opposite side of the field from goal to midfield. This means there are always two officials, the referee and one linesman, close to the action and watching it from opposite sides. This is the system used almost everywhere around the world, except in Russia and some of the Iron Curtain countries. There the referee stays near one sideline and away from the middle of play, with the senior linesman on the other side of the field acting as a deputy.

Linesmen serve only to designate the team that gets the ball when it goes out of bounds and function strictly in a consultive capacity as far as penalties are concerned. The big decision is made by the referee alone and cannot be questioned.

Back in 1889 soccer was under the control of two umpires,

one in each half of the field, and the referee was only called on when these two could not agree. This worked badly and by 1891 the referee was put in supreme control of the game and the umpires became linesmen. In the 1930's the British experimented timidly with two referees but after a few games it was determined that a match could only be controlled properly by one man.

The soccer referee has a peculiar method of showing his displeasure with a player. He pulls a little book out of his pocket, asks the man his name (even though he probably knows it) and solemnly writes it down. This is called "pulling the book" on a player. In international level soccer the book can be pulled three times and then a player is ejected from the game. The English allow four cautions before dismissing anyone, and this rule has been followed by the National Professional Soccer League and the United Soccer Association.

When a player in any country is put out of the game, the referee sends a report to the national football association, or, in the case of the American professional leagues, to the commissioner. The player may appeal, but if he does not, disciplinary action is compulsory and must be accepted. In England he can be fined up to £100 ($240) or suspended for as much as twenty-eight days.

In recent years even English referees have become concerned with the rowdyism of the fans. In 1967 hooligans attacked the referees at two top league games, Nottingham Forest-Manchester City and Tottenham Hotspur-Sunderland. At a Leeds-Liverpool match seven fans were arrested when they rushed onto the field after a penalty kick had been awarded. So disturbed was the League Referees' Association that there was talk of going on strike for a single Saturday and Alan Hardaker, secretary of the English League, declared "I for one would not blame them. If I were a referee I would be sick to death of this kind of behavior. Fans need to be reeducated to accept decisions that go against their team."

Police patrols were strengthened as a result of the outbreaks, and barricades were put up in some parks around the goal area to protect the goalkeeper.

Despite the occupational hazards, the meager pay, and the lack of security, there is no shortage of referees around the world. In England alone there are more than 16,000 qualified referees: 3,000 in Class 1, 5,000 in Class 2, and 8,000 in Class 3. Those in the first two classes are termed senior referees and from this group about eight hundred are recommended by the county associations. The Football League then selects about four hundred of these, of which eighty or ninety become referees in the four top league divisions and the balance serve as linesmen. Even to get in the main group of 16,000, a candidate must pass the written tests of a strict Football Examination Board.

In addition to all his other responsibilities, the referee in soccer is the sole timekeeper of the game. Everywhere, except in American professional soccer, timekeeping is a very private matter. Only the referee knows exactly when the game will end, because it is his decision alone when to take time out in case of serious injuries or other interruptions of play, and he keeps his stopwatch carefully screened from the inquisitive eyes of players. Spectators who use their own watches know approximately when each half is nearing an end, but the shrill whistle of the referee always comes as something of a surprise. Since the stadiums used for professional soccer in the United States and Canada are used for football and baseball, electric countdown clocks are available with dials that measure off fifteen minutes. These are put into operation one quarter hour from the end of each half but even here the time is unofficial and usually does not coincide with the referee's own private watch.

Refereeing in soccer has produced its full share of colorful characters. One of the most famous at the start of the century in England was Jack Howcroft, a firm disciplinarian who wore a black hat and had a habit of wagging a warning finger under an offender's nose. He retired in 1925 at the age of fifty. Shortly before leaving the game he became worried over approaching age and in an effort to look younger he shaved off his flowing moustache. In his next game the players failed to recognize him and started taking liberties with what they thought was an inexperienced official. He dealt out a penalty with all his majesty and the culprit recognized his voice.

"Great Scott, it's Mr. 'Owcroft," the player squealed and the game proceeded without further shenanigans.

More recently the "King" of the soccer pitch is considered to be Arthur Ellis, whose hour of greatest trial came in the World Cup in Berne, Switzerland, where he presided over a game between Hungary and Brazil, nations that take their soccer in deadly earnest. So vicious was it that he sent two Brazilians and one Hungarian to the sidelines and the game ended with only nineteen players on the field—an unprecedented act of discipline.

Poor pay, abuse, even physical danger have their compensations. As Walter Crossley said of refereeing a Cup Final in vast Wembley Stadium, "You have butterflies in your stomach when you walk out but when your feet hit the turf you feel like a million."

9

Great personalities of the game

———◆———

Like every sport, major or minor, soccer has a full list of celebrated performers. Unlike track or swimming, where exact times and distances prove that the young men and women of the 1960's are much faster and stronger than their predecessors fifty years ago, soccer has no convenient yardstick by which greatness can be measured. Even baseball, American football, and basketball are crammed with statistics that can be used to bolster arguments over respective merits. In soccer there is only one valid statistic and that is goals scored. Since these are few and far between and since only the forward wall is involved in the act, great midfield and defensive players tend to go unrewarded, except for the goalkeeper, who can take pride in the exact number of times he has averted a score.

Any roll call of soccer's great names must start with Stanley Matthews of England, the only soccer player in the world to be knighted by a Queen and a rarity among all athletes in strenuous sports in that he was still a star at forty and able to play with the best at fifty.

A mild, smallish, sharp-faced man, he had great dribbling skill, with tremendous acceleration from a standing position. He was also a scrupulously law-abiding player. His father, Jack, was a professional boxer and wanted young Matthews to follow him in the ring, but the boy's heart was always set on soccer. For a while there was considerable strain in the household but finally the father gave in, insisting, however, that the boy prove his worth by being chosen for an international team. Stanley did. When he was only fourteen he was selected for England's schoolboy team that played Wales. England won 4–1.

Matthews joined Stoke City at fifteen as an office boy and first played as an amateur. At seventeen he signed with Stoke City as a professional, receiving £5 per week during the season and £3 in the off-season—with a £10 bonus for signing, too. Ahead of him lay a dazzling career that spanned more than thirty years and which finally brought him the distinction of being invited to Buckingham Palace in 1965, where Queen Elizabeth II named him Sir Stanley Matthews.

His greatest quality was his ability to rise to a dramatic occasion, as he proved in 1953 in his third and last Cup Final at Wembley. He was then thirty-eight years old and an injury to his right leg had kept him out of play for three months. An operation mended matters and as his Blackpool team edged closer to the Cup Final, sentiment built in England behind Matthews, who in his two previous Cup Final appearances had been on the losing side and now obviously was in the twilight of his great career. When the semifinals determined that it would be Blackpool against the Bolton Wanderers at Wembley, newspapers started calling it "The Stanley Matthews Final" and soccer fans, except for a few Bolton diehards, were pulling for Matthews to win a Cup medal at last.

Never did a sentimental favorite appear more doomed. At the half Bolton led 2–1, and in the 55th minute forged into what looked like an unbeatable 3–1 lead. With only 23 minutes to

81

go. Stan Mortensen scored for Blackpool to make it 3–2. Still Matthews' cause looked almost hopeless.

"I pulled every trick I knew," he said afterwards. These were numerous. He was all over the field, throwing the defense off balance, eluding tacklers, and dribbling as only he could. With only three minutes left Matthews set up a goal that Mortensen scored, and it was a tie game.

Wembley and its 100,000 was in a pandemonium. With only one minute left to play, Matthews got the ball and charged down the sidelines, shaking off every opponent, until finally he was in a position to send a pass to a teammate in front of the nets.

At this critical moment he realized he was standing in a divot hole in the usually immaculate turf of Wembley. He said afterwards he felt as if an unseen hand held him up. He kicked and fell to the ground in pain. The mighty roar told him the goal had been scored; Blackpool had won 4–3, and at long last he had his coveted medal.

"Well done," said the Queen as she handed it to him.

Probably the finest description of how Matthews played soccer can be found in *The Great Ones,* by Joe Mercer, himself one of the game's greats:

"I had Stanley Matthews trapped against the corner flag at Stoke. His back was practically touching the post and I was within a yard of him. I thought: 'Got you! This time I've got you!'

"Ten times, probably, he had beaten me in that game. He would bring the ball squarely to me so that I would never know whether he would go inside or outside with it. He would lean so far that it would be obvious it had to go that way—but his balance is so perfect he would then sway and go the other way.

"However, I had been working on a plan, pushing him up the wing all the time, and now I knew that he could not trick me. I was rather fit and fast at that time. So I moved in—and broke my thumb on the post!

"What he did, how he got away, I will never know. Johnny Carey, the versatile Manchester United player, used to say: 'Playing Stan is like playing a ghost.' It was an apt description."

At the top of the list of the active stars of the 1960–70 decade stands Edson Arantes de Nascimento, better known simply as Pelé. No one knows what he earns from his construction and rubber product businesses, to which he has now added the art of folk-song writing, but guesses range from $200,000 to $750,000 yearly. Even his soccer salary is substantial. Pelé, who reached age 27 on October 23, 1967, shortly thereafter signed a three-year contract for $4,500 per month with Sao Paulo's Santos Club.

Pelé is a Brazilian institution. Offers of several million dollars have been made by European clubs desiring to purchase him, but Pelé is not for sale. He probably would not emigrate even if he were sold, and as Brazilians say, one sure cause of a revolution in Brazil would be his sale to another country.

"I only play for three teams: Santos, the Sao Paulo state selection, and the Brazilian national team," he says. Pelé holds the world record for scores, having made more than a thousand in the ten years since he first appeared as an international player at the age of seventeen.

Pelé caught the eye of a soccer scout, Waldemir deBrito, when he was eleven, playing in a pickup game with construction workers.

"Of all the players in that game only one stood out," said DeBrito. "I immediately spotted what can be called genius."

For four years DeBrito worked with Pelé until finally he was ready for a professional tryout. DeBrito modestly introduced him to Santos officials: "I want you to meet the player who will one day be the greatest in the world."

Pelé scrimmaged, and was immediately signed for $75 a

month. In his first game, won by Santos 7–1, he scored four goals and the following year, when only sixteen, he was named to the Brazilian national team. In the 1958 World Cup he made the first of a series of spectacular goals in top-flight soccer. His back to the nets, he lobbed a kick over his head against the body of a Welsh opponent, wheeled, and booted home a goal before the ball could touch the turf.

Pelé is a compact, dark-skinned flash of lightning. He can better 10 flat for 100 yards, and in soccer shoes he can run away from almost any other player in the world. When he gets control of the ball there seems to be no way to pry it loose from him, not even by the most vicious tackle or feet-first slide.

Some of the goals he has scored are legends in Brazil. There was the time in 1961 while playing for his own club, Santos, that he took a pass in his own half of the field, dribbled past seven opponents, eluded the goalkeeper, and scored. Then in 1962 when the Brazilian national team won the World Cup by defeating Mexico 2–1, Pelé scooted half the length of the field, reversed himself and outsmarted two defending backs to loft the ball into the upper corner of the nets. In Brazil's first game in the 1966 World Cup play in England, Pelé was awarded a penalty kick against Bulgaria just outside the penalty area. Although four sturdy Bulgarians locked arms in front of the goal to form a seemingly unpenetrable barrier, Pelé hooked the ball around them into the nets. Brazil won 2–0 but it was a costly victory. Pelé was set upon so hard by the Bulgarians that he did not play again in the Cup competition and Brazil's chances of retaining its world championship went glimmering. Brazil took the defeat hard. Police had to guard the home of Vicente Feola, the Brazilian coach, to keep incendiaries away.

Wherein lies his genius? His ability to control the ball while running at top speed is one factor. His powerful kicking is another. His incredibly accurate heading is a third. But the incalculable factor is the personal magnetism that accounts for vast crowds wherever he plays, such as the 41,598 that went to Yankee Stadium in 1966 to see him. The next year only a few thousand less showed up, despite a rainy day.

If Pelé is the king of world soccer in the 1960's, then Eusebio is the crown prince. His full name is Eusebio da Silva Ferreira, and he was born in 1943 in Portuguese East Africa. He reached a pinnacle of soccer glory in the 1966 World Cup in England when he won the bonus of £1,000 as individual high scorer with nine goals in six games—four of them scored against the surprisingly strong North Koreans who led the Portuguese national team 3–0 until Eusebio, the Black Panther, started firing. Portugal won 5–3 and the only goal Eusebio did not score came after a corner kick by him.

Eusebio is one of soccer's deadliest kickers. He scored thirty-nine consecutive penalty shots and when his string was finally broken he immediately congratulated the goalkeeper and asked him for his autograph.

Born in poverty, he signed first as a professional with the Sporting Club of Lourenco Marques and received as a bonus new soccer shoes. He had never before had a pair. He wept for joy. At nineteen he was purchased by Benefica of Portugal and immediately broke into the starting lineup, an amazing feat considering that Benefica had just won the European Cup of Champions. He has played on every Portuguese national team (formed by selecting the best players from all the professional teams in the country) since then, and in the World Cup in 1966 he was virtually responsible for Portugal's third-place finish. No one knows his value; Benefica rejected an offer of $500,000 for him from the Vasco da Gama team of Sao Paulo, Brazil, seeking a counterattraction to Pelé.

When he was in the United States in 1966 for an exhibition game he dazzled Andy Robustelli, coach of the Continental League's Brooklyn football Dodgers, by punting sixty yards with ease and by sending one place kick between the goalposts from nearly sixty-five yards out.

Another of the game's greats, Ferenc (Pancho) Puskas, a

tubby Hungarian with a left foot that can propel a soccer ball into the net at incredible speed, was signed for 1968 by the San Francisco Golden Gales of the United Soccer Association. When the Gales merged with the Vancouver Royals, Puskas went to Vancouver as part of the deal. His salary as Royals' player-coach was estimated at more than $50,000 and in acquiring him the Royals got a player who had what everyone agreed was something North American soccer needed most— a name, a personality, a style of play that could capture the imagination of fans. Even if no longer capable of going a full game at top speed, he was still able in his forties to break up any soccer match with a single, brilliant burst.

Puskas, sometimes known as the "galloping major," came to the Royals via the Hungarian Revolution of 1956 and more directly from the famous Real Madrid club. Real Madrid reputedly outbid Inter of Milan for his services, by $300,000 to $200,000 after he fled Budapest with his wife, Elizabeth, and their daughter, Aniko.

Puskas began playing soccer at eleven and through special governmental permit he was allowed at eighteen to join the top Hungarian team, Kispet. When Hungary chose its national team on the usual all-star basis Puskas was included by virtue of scoring seven goals in the first two games he played with Kispet, and he remained on Hungary's great international teams until the Revolution. In 1953 he captained the Hungarians in a stunning 6–3 victory over England in Wembley Stadium.

His career at Real Madrid was equally brilliant. Six times in nine years, with Puskas and Alfredo di Stefano as the driving forces, Real was European champion and once was world champion.

His father had been a player-coach, and it was this combination of opportunities in San Francisco that lured him from Madrid. He entered his new job with supreme confidence: "In five years the Gales will be known in Europe and all over the world."

Alfredo di Stefano, like Puskas, came to Real Madrid from abroad. His career started in 1947 with River Plate of Argentina and came to an end in 1967 when he made a short appearance in a testimonial match between Real Madrid and Celtic of Glasgow. In 622 matches played in Spain he scored 460 goals. Real Madrid bought him from River Plate in 1953 for the comparatively modest sum of $67,000 and launched him on his way to stardom.

He was called the White Arrow and played a deep center forward, setting up attacks from midfield, and frequently cracking home the goals himself. In European Cup games he scored forty-nine times, a record that no one has approached.

Di Stefano's bald head made him conspicuous on a field of bushy-haired youngsters. One of his most famous games was the European Cup final against Eintracht Frankfurt of West Germany in 1960 in Glasgow's Hampden Park stadium. In that classic, Di Stefano scored three goals in Real's 7–3 victory and one of them Scottish fans will never forget. Frankfurt had just scored and Di Stefano kicked off from the center circle. He tapped the ball to his inside right, Luis del Sol, took the return pass still in the center circle, went forward two paces, and sent the ball whistling into the nets, half the length of the field.

Danny Branchflower may not belong among the all-time greats of soccer, although his credentials are substantial. As captain of the Tottenham Hotspurs he led his team to the First Division championship, and also to victory in the Cup Final, 2–0 over Leicester City in 1960–61, a "double" that because of its rarity is reverentially regarded in England. But his impact on American television was nothing less than startling. His commentary on National Professional Soccer League games was like nothing heard over the air before: caustic criticism of ineptness and faulty strategy with almost a minimum of praise for good play. American audiences, accustomed either to a bland description of the action or an enthusiastic hometown partisanship that excuses all misplays, were amused, bewildered, but always interested.

Branchflower, who had long nourished a hope of getting into journalism or radio-TV broadcasting once his active career was ended, has always been a maverick. Born of poor parents in Belfast, Northern Ireland on February 10, 1926, he started playing soccer in the streets. When World War II started he joined the R.A.F. Training Corps, which led to a special scholarship at St. Andrew's University in Scotland. He was in Canada waiting to be assigned to the Far East when the war ended. Back home he wavered between soccer and St. Andrew's, but decided in favor of soccer. He signed as a professional with Glentoran for a £50 bonus and £3 per week—and was highly irked to learn that others signed for £500 and £10 per week. Each season he argued with the directors over his wages and finally was promised one third of the transfer fee if he was sold by Glentoran provided he would sign again for only £5 per week and a £20 bonus. Barnsley in England wanted him and the directors (not the same ones who had made the promise of one third of the transfer fee) said all they could give him out of the sale was £700. He found out later that the transfer fee was £6,000. Eventually he got into a hot argument with the Barnsley manager over being allowed to practice whenever he wished with a soccer ball. It was just not being done, so he asked for a transfer. He was sold for £15,000 to Aston Villa, unusually high for a wing half.

Soon he showed his rugged independence at Aston Villa. On an international trip to Canada he ran into a new soccer system that interested him: the 3–3–4 lineup, or three fullbacks, three halfbacks, and four forwards. He tried to introduce it at Aston Village but the experimentation, he felt, was timid. Realizing that Aston Villa was getting nowhere, he asked again for a transfer and finally landed with the Spurs in 1954. This opened up London with its exciting communications possibilities, and from there the trail led to American microphones.

Joe Mercer summed up his rugged individualism:

"Danny was always a positive player, though he had to achieve success before he was accepted . . . He had no negative thoughts in his mind; he was original and positive in his approach to the game. 'Let the other team worry about us; we will be creative!'—this was his creed and he was a great artist."

As baseball has its Casey Stengel, soccer has its Matt Busby. Like Casey, Busby was only an ordinary player, and again like Casey, he achieved his real fame as a manager. World War II was the dividing line in his career. Prior to the War he had played for Manchester City and was signed by Liverpool shortly before the hostilities. In 1945 Liverpool wanted him back as coach, but Harold Hardman, chairman of Manchester United, the rundown rival of Manchester City, thought he saw genius in the bubbly, mild-mannered Scotsman. He was right.

Almost at once Busby transformed Manchester United into a soccer power. In the next two decades, while 640 managers came and went with other English teams, Busby stayed on and on at Manchester United. Three times he had to rebuild the team—the first time because his players got too old, and the second time in 1958 when the bulk of his team lost their lives in an airplane crash in Munich. The third rebuilding was also because his players had grown too old.

Yet England almost lost him to the United States. While he was still in his teens Busby's mother decided to emigrate to the United States, where so many of her family had gone after loss of their menfolk in World War I. Busby applied for a visa and was told it would take six months. So he went to work in the mines where his father had worked before him. He hated the work. Busby also played hard at soccer, and skillfully. Soon he received and accepted, to the regret of his mother who saw her plans of going to America fading away, a professional offer from Manchester City.

89

In 1957 Busby's Manchester United team, known for obvious reasons as "Busby's Babes," had the Cup Final in its grasp but lost it to Aston Villa 2–0 because of an accident in the opening moments of the game. Aston Villa's Peter McParland had headed the ball straight into the arms of the Manchester United goalie, Ray Wood, who stood trying to make up his mind what to do. At that moment McParland unexpectedly charged him, so hard that both players fell stunned to the ground. Wood suffered a broken jaw. Under the no-substitution rule he tried to play out the game at right wing but suffered from blackouts. Jackie Branchflower took over as goalie. McParland scored both of Aston Villa's points, leading to the cynical comment that he "got two goals and a goalkeeper." Busby argued persuasively after the game that substitutes should be allowed in such circumstances, and that goalies should have better protection from rough play.

An insight into his shrewdness in handling players was shown when he bought Tommy Taylor from Barnsley. Long negotiations finally came to a head when Joe Richards, the Barnsley chairman, said Busby could have Taylor for a £30,000 transfer fee.

"You know how big fees have affected players in the past," Busby declared. "And that £30,000 transfer tag could so easily ruin Tommy Taylor if it preyed on his mind. Would you accept £29,999 instead?"

Richards did.

Busby had one great asset aside from his knowledge of the game—the ability to persuade his management to spend freely for the players he wanted. Manchester United set a British record transfer fee in paying $350,000 for Denis Law, and in 1966 paid $180,000 for a goalie, Alex Stepney.

Under Busby, United has won five league championships and four Cup Finals. Like Casey Stengel, Busby is a superb judge of young players and interest is high in English soccer circles to see if his latest find, Brian Kidd, can step into the

90

shoes of Denis Law. In England Busby's name is synonymous with soccer football.

The list of soccer's colorful personalities is endless. There was Alex Jackson, who had no zest for training but was reputed to have laid £5 to £1,000 early in one season that his team, Huddersfield Town, would win the Cup Final and that he would score in every round. He missed scoring in the Final by a head shot that grazed the post and Huddersfield Town lost— but up to that point the bet, if it was a bet, was viable. Jackson died in a war accident in Egypt. There was Alex James, who had a shambling walk and looked deceptively small but was an absolute master of a soccer ball; Bill Meredith, who, like Sir Stanley Matthews, played into his fiftieth year; and Alex Morton, who played thirty times for Scotland against England. It is legitimate to wonder: Will American names someday be inscribed on the roster of soccer immortals?

10

The violent fan; soccer's tragedies

———◆———

Something there is about soccer that brings out the brute in spectators. Even in New York, where sports events are taken calmly (except for fight fans, who may toss bottles after unpopular decisions), soccer has sparked outbursts starting with Bill Cox's International Soccer League at Randall's Island and extending even to venerable Yankee Stadium. There in 1967 twoscore aficionados of the Cagliari team of Sardinia chased the referee, Leo Goldstein of Brooklyn, around the infield. One even succeeded in punching Goldstein in the nose before he could reach the safety of a baseball dugout.

As is almost always the case in soccer it was a decision, or the lack of one, by the referee that ignited the outburst. Early in the game between Cagliari, representing Chicago in the United Soccer Association, and Cerro of Montevideo, Uruguay, representing New York, Ruben Gonzalez of the New York side collided with Communardo Niccolai of Chicago so hard that two stitches were needed to repair the gash in Niccolai's head. Then with only three minutes left to play, New York's Rose

Rotolo knocked Niccolai down again. Niccolai's teammates pushed Rotolo and exchanged unpleasantries with Goldstein. Fans crowded closer and closer to the playing field. Finally one jumped the fence and the donnybrook was on. Goldstein, at least, was able to kick one of his detractors in the chest and finally special policemen restored order.

Afterwards Anthony DiGiovanni, head of the stadium's special police detail, said bluntly, "Those fans were animals. But my men did the right thing by not leaving their posts to make arrests or stop isolated fighting on the field when it first started. If they had, there would have been a thousand people on the field."

The cause of the storm was the feeling that Goldstein should have thrown Gonzalez and Rotolo out of the game, a view that Goldstein did not share. Goldstein is one of the best-known of American officials and among his international assignments was the World Cup in Chile in 1962.

Shaken by the experiment, Goldstein exclaimed afterwards, "With all my heart I feel that I refereed a good game. And this is what I get for my efforts." But the Cagliari coach, Manilio Scopigno, thought otherwise: "The referee lost control of the game."

It was the same Scopigno who only forty-eight hours later in Toronto led his team off the field, with nine minutes left to play, when the Toronto City team, the Hibernians of Edinburgh, went ahead of Cagliari 2–1 by quickly capitalizing on a free kick. The Cagliari players pushed Referee Art King and were joined in their scuffling by Scopigno. When they quit the game it was an open invitation to several thousand of their Italian sympathizers in join in the melee. They did. King was kicked and punched before police could rescue him. Four of the brawlers were taken into protective custody but no charges were made.

Dick Walsh, commissioner of the United Soccer Association, took a dim view of the outbreak. He blamed the Cagliari management, and full reports were forwarded both to FIFA and the governing body of Italian soccer. As a result the Italian League's disciplinary committee voted to withhold seventy percent of one month's salary from sixteen of the players. Scopigno was dismissed by his Sardinian club.

A fight between two players, Dotti of Inter Milan and Tonhino of Santos, Brazil, set off a twelve-minute riot at Yankee Stadium August 27, 1967. It took fifty New York City policemen to put it down. Referee Olten Ayres Abreu, a Brazilian, had called a penalty kick against Inter, which was leading 1–0 with thirteen minutes left to play. About 150 pro-Italian fans poured onto the field and started scuffling with the Santos players, the referee, and special policemen trying to preserve order. In one side issue a half dozen white-suited Santos players chased a red-shirted Inter fan half across the Yankee outfield and were ready to pounce on him when he slipped and fell. Quickly a score of Inter partisans dashed up to protect him. The Inter manager wisely waved his players off the field and took them to their lockers. Two of the brawling players were ejected from the game, order was restored, and Inter went on to win by a lone goal, avenging the previous year's 4–1 defeat by Santos and gaining thereby the United States Cup. A crowd of 37,063 had shown up to see the great Pelé, but he played only the first half, serving mostly as a decoy as tall Italians kept him surrounded.

It was a key decision by a referee that in 1964 touched off the worst riot in sports annals, resulting in the death of 309 persons and injuries to one thousand more. The scene was the national stadium in Lima, Peru, where amateur teams of Argentina and Peru were competing for a place in the Olympic Games soccer tournament. Argentina led 1–0 with less than two minutes to play, at which point a Peruvian wingman kicked a goal which would have tied the score except that the Uruguayan referee, R. Angel Pazos, ordered it nullified because of rough play on the part of Peru.

94

The Peruvian players protested vehemently but the game was resumed. Then a man entered the field and chased the referee. He was arrested. He was followed by another, a sports enthusiast known in the city as Bomba. The police tripped him and an officer hit him on the back of the neck. This incensed the crowd in the south section of the stadium where the cheapest standing-room admissions are sold. Stones and bottles were thrown at the police. By now the crowd on the field had swollen to more than a hundred and the stadium was in an uproar.

The police resorted to tear gas in an effort to restore order. A stampede started in the north stand, also a low-priced admission area. In scarcely two minutes the north stand emptied. But the steel doors at the exits that should have been opened as the game drew to its close were locked tight. Waves of humanity pressed against the barriers. When the gates were finally opened from the outside bodies were piled against them, row on row. Most of the crowd of 50,000 watched in helpless horror.

Once the violence started, it spread swiftly. Angry fans smashed all the windows in the stadium. They sacked stores and overturned cars in nearby streets. They set buildings afire and when the police finally established order, the government proclaimed a state of emergency throughout Peru.

Many of those killed were trampled to death. A peculiar aspect of soccer stadiums accounted for some of the fatalities. In the sections where there are no seats and the audience stands there are curving steel fences consisting of single bars about waist high, known as crash barriers. Many were killed when they were pinned against the bars as the crowd surged down from above. In one of the ugliest developments in this tragedy, toughs stole wallets, rings, and watches from the bodies of the dead and unconscious.

Women and children were among the victims but most of the dead and injured were men of the working class. The government later granted small pensions to the families of persons who died in the disaster.

In the heart of the city some 1,000 students of the Federation of University Students rioted in the University Plaza, demanding the resignation of Juan Languasco, the Interior Minister who controls the police. The students were angry because mounted police had helped bring the mob under control and four deaths were attributed to police bullets.

A police detail at the stadium rushed the referee and the players to safety in the locker room and then spirited them away in a bus. It is safe to assume that if the local partisans could have laid hands on the referee and the Argentinian team they would have been lynched.

Argentina was adjudged the winner of the game, and went to the Olympics in Japan but fared poorly, being tied by Ghana 1–1 in the first round and losing to Japan 3–2.

A soccer riot second only to the 1964 disaster in Lima occurred September 17, 1967, in Kayseri, Turkey, and as usual the spark that touched it off was a referee's decision. In this case a disputed goal was allowed for Kayseri against Sivas, a rival town 110 miles way. In all forty-one died and six hundred were injured, but while some perished in the stampede, many were killed as the result of the use of stones, knives, and even pistols.

Sivas had brought along 5,000 fans and they made known their displeasure loudly when Kayseri scored after twenty minutes of play. The local fans reacted strongly, and significantly thirty-eight of the dead were residents of Sivas. Turkish and Kayseri policemen, with bayonets fixed to their rifles, brought the crowd of 30,000 under control and the Turkish cabinet, meeting in emergency session, temporarily suspended all games in the Second Turkish Soccer League in which the two teams played. The bodies of the dead Sivas fans were flown home in a Turkish air force transport. Thousands attended the mass funeral.

The rivalry between Kayseria and Sivas first became tense three years earlier when another match ended with a fight in the stands in which eleven were injured.

Lest anyone think that emotions run high only in Latin America or the Middle East let him consider Glasgow, one of the northernmost citadels of soccer. Glasgow has two redoubtable teams, the Celtics, which won the coveted European Cup in 1967, and the Rangers, which lost the Cup Winners' Cup by one goal in overtime to Bayern Munich in Nuremberg. Most of the Celtics' followers are Roman Catholic, most of Rangers' Protestant. Numerous riots verging on holy wars have marked their annual game, although Glasgow casualties have never reached the proportions of those in Lima and Kayseri.

To curb emotions in 1967, Glasgow police warned that any spectator wearing his team's colors would be arrested. Every man who went through the turnstiles was frisked for bottles or anything else that could be used as a weapon. Five hundred policemen were assigned to the game and they herded Ranger fans together on the terraces at one end of the field, and Celtic fans on terraces at the other. Despite these precautions, police had to arrest nine troublemakers and sixteen persons were taken to hospitals. Some became emotionally ill just watching the game and others were hit by flying bottles that somehow got smuggled in. Two rowdies caught scuffling in the street declared they were Ranger fans and resented being spat upon by Celtics from the top of a bus. The upshot of it all was that the game ended in a 2–2 tie, and by virtue of this the Celtics won the Scottish League title on total points.

Even the normally antiseptic 1967 Pan-American Games in Winnipeg were not free from the threat of violence. "Cuba, go home," the crowd shouted as Canada defeated Fidel Castro's squad 2–1. A Cuban retaliated as the match neared its end by launching a haymaker that knocked Canada's Karl Kauch to the ground. In the melee that followed some of the red, white, and blue-shirted men who came along with the Cuban team in order to keep an eye on the athletes dashed on the field. Their cartridge belts were visible but no guns were flashed. And so rough was the play in the Pan-American tournament that two players on each side were expelled from the Colombia–Argentina game, and no less than four from the Colombian team in the match against Mexico, at the end of which Referee Ken Dunstan was escorted from the field by police. But the tournament came to a happy climax when Mexico won the championship by defeating Bermuda 4–0 before a crowd of 16,000, largest ever to see a soccer game in Winnipeg.

Nor are the stolid Swiss immune. In a recent Swiss Soccer Cup Final won by Basel over Lausanne 2–1, rioting erupted so fiercely that the referee had to call the game three minutes from the end and sprint for his life to the dressing room.

Even in staid England things got to the point where, in 1964, the Council of the English Football Association, the ruling body of the sport, in an effort to curb rowdyism urged team managers and coaches to sit in the stands and not give advice to players from the touchline, and called on club directors to ease pressure on coaches and players to win at all costs.

"Success is not as important as presenting an interesting spectacle which will attract supporters, without whom the game will cease to exist at the professional level," said the Council.

Rowdyism at English soccer matches appeared to be spreading in 1967 and the Birmingham City club, in a bold effort to keep the fans under control, resorted not to more police as might be expected, but rather to twelve well-rounded models from London who were dressed in mini-skirts and paraded around the grounds before the game and at the half.

"No one could be bored with so much leg about," said the Birmingham City promotion manager, David Exall. "I am sure they will watch these girls and behave themselves."

But David Wiseman, a member of the English Football Association and vice-chairman of Birmingham City, did not like it at all: "Display like this should not take place under any circumstances on a football ground."

Going even further, Dr. John Harrington, the psychiatrist who has been asked by the English Minister of Sport to try to figure out what causes soccer rowdyism and how it can be cured, warned that scantily clad, curvaceous girls might have the opposite effect intended. He declared: "Soccer is a male occasion and the effect on the crowd of mainly young men left in the state of excitement and suddenly faced with a visual stimulation of a different kind will not necessarily be calming."

Because of the Latin-American tendency to attack hated referees or teams or both, playing fields south of the border are usually circled with a high fence and sometimes even a moat. The security precautions at the world's largest arena, the Municipal Stadium of Rio de Janiero, are impregnable. Between the stands—which can accommodate 125,000 in seats and 30,000 standing, and with a little crowding can hold 200,000—and the playing field there is a moat nine feet wide and sixteen feet deep which is filled with water before every game. As a final precaution, the doors to the players' dressing rooms, located under the field and approached from within the moat, are made of heavy steel and can be closed rapidly if trouble develops.

Overwrought emotions are not always confined to the spectators. Fights on the field are not uncommon and in the 1954 World Cup in Stockholm, the Brazilians and Hungarians had it out in their dressing rooms. Hungary had defeated Brazil 4–2 in a rough game and this without the services of its injured super-star, Puskas. When the Hungarian players marched triumphantly to their quarters they found the Brazilian team lying in wait. Flying fists and bottles sent half a dozen to the hospital.

Students of mass emotions have yet to come up with a clear answer as to why soccer seems to inspire violence. Because of the increase of hooliganism in England, Dr. John Harrington, who frowned on mini-skirts as a cure for the problem, is at work on the problem at government's request. He found in soccer crowds signs of "hypnotic trance" and "frightening aggression" but took comfort in the fact most Englishmen discharge their aggressions with bad language.

The question has even been raised whether British sportsmanship, always considered the 24-karat standard, has been alloyed. The London Sports Writers Association, facing up to the menace, decided in 1967 to make the Celtics of Glasgow ineligible for its award of sportsman of the year because of the way the Scots played in a game against the Racing Club of Argentina in Montevideo, Uruguay, a game in which four Celtics were expelled for rough tactics.

"The voting," said the sportswriters primly, "is restricted to those who have contributed most to Great Britain's international sporting prestige."

Elsewhere distinguished experts also sought an answer. Professor Francesco Ferraroti, a Rome University sociologist, analyzed the fans this way: "Their frustration when the heroes they identify with are being 'robbed' gives rise to a mob psychology that I think is quite similar to the lynching psychology."

The English Football Association mulled over statistics on another aspect of fan violence, namely, the number of disciplinary offenses on the part of players, which are in themselves frequently a cause of crowd outbreaks. Said the *F.A. News* in an editorial: "It is held in some quarters that ill discipline on the field provokes ill discipline off the field." It analyzed first division offenses to show that 294 of the 361 reported in the 1966–67 season were dealt with on the field in the form of cautions, and 67 were reported to the disciplinary committee. The offenders were suspended, censured, or fined. Out of the 67 cases, "27 could be directly attributable to physical violence."

Violence has also beset the game of soccer quite apart from

100

the wrath of partisans. In 1902 part of the grandstand collapsed at Ibrox Park in Glasgow in a match between England and Scotland and twenty-five people were killed and more than five hundred injured. Even worse was the disaster on March 9, 1946, at Burnden Park, Bolton, where thirty-three were killed and more than four hundred injured when the crash barriers broke. The crowd was so packed together that the fatalities were from suffocation and crushing. Every available inch of space in the stadium was filled. The match was between the Bolton Wanderers and Stoke City with its fabulous Stanley Matthews. The tragedy occurred in one corner of the grounds and was not immediately apparent to the players or the other spectators. When the players finally realized what had happened they wanted to stop the game. The referee, however, feared the news might cause a panic among the rest of the crowd and ordered the game to go on in what must be considered one of the stiffest exhibitions of British stiff-upper-lip-manship.

But from the English point of view, the greatest tragedy in soccer occurred February 5, 1958, in Munich when an airplane carrying the great Manchester United team failed to become airborne after three attempts in a snowstorm, and crashed, killing twenty-three persons. Eight of these were players and eight were British sportswriters.

The team was on its way home after tying Yugoslavia 3–3 and thereby advancing to the semifinals of the European Cup tournament. Manchester United had been a Football Association Cup finalist the previous two years and was probably the most valuable collection of soccer players in the world. On the soccer market the team would have brought close to $1,000,000 in transfer fees. Manchester as a city went into mourning and Queen Elizabeth and President Tito of Yugoslavia sent messages of condolence.

Among those who lost their lives was Duncan Edwards,

101

already a star at twenty and on his way to becoming one of soccer's immortals. His kicking was astounding. Twice during his short career he scored goals by driving the ball so hard into the arms of the goalie that it carried him back into the nets. Among his tricks was the ability to kick a ball ten yards away from him, at which point it would bounce and then return to his feet. The survivors included Matt Busby, the team manager, one of soccer's masterminds. He suffered severe chest injuries and the physicians had to work long and hard to save him.

Soccer has no provision for restocking teams hit by disasters, unlike American professional football and baseball which set up plans early in the flying age to deal with such emergencies through a pool of players.

The worst of all soccer air disasters occurred in 1949 when the entire thirteen-man Italian championship team of Turino was wiped out. They were returning home from a victory over Portugal's national team when the plane, beset by a heavy rainstorm as it neared the Turin airport, brushed against the cathedral of Turin and fell in flames. Turino held the Italian championship for the previous four years and was awarded in death its fifth title.

Among those who perished was Valentino Mazzola, considered one of soccer's all-time finest. Waiting at the airport for him was his wife, Emilia, and his seven-year-old son, Sandro.

"I couldn't believe it," Sandro said long afterwards. "This was my father and it couldn't be true."

Sandro, brought up with the game, joined the Inter team of Milan after getting the college degree his father's heart had been set on for him.

One of the strangest of all soccer accidents took the life of Luciano J. Fernandez of Portugal's great Benefica team and almost cost that of the super-star, Eusebio. The two were among seven players relaxing in a new communal bath equipped with a whirlpool machine. A passerby turned on the switch and a

102

short circuit electrocuted Fernandez and knocked Eusebio unconscious. Jaime Graca, another of the players, managed to jump out of the water and shut off the machine or the casualties might have been more numerous.

But soccer has survived all these disasters and around the world the enthusiasm for the sport continues to grow.

11

The impact of the lush American
salary and pension structure on
the generally underpaid
soccer player

———◆———

The American professional athlete is without doubt the most security-minded performer in the world. The four major professional sports—baseball, football, hockey, and basketball—all have opulent pension schemes for their players, of which the most lavish is baseball's. The standard approach of a club wanting to sign a young boy is more apt to be "Play with us and you will earn a big salary and a pension that will take care of you for the rest of your life" than "How glorious it is to wear a Yankee uniform."

What, then, will result from the exposure of foreign players to the lush American salary and pension structure? Without doubt the cross-fertilization of ideas will give entrenched club managements across the ocean some anxious moments.

England has started to tackle the problem. The betting pools now make a contribution to the Football Association which amounts to nine percent of a soccer player's salary in the four top divisions. This is known as the Provident Scheme and when a player reaches thirty-five—or retires from soccer, if it is after thirty-five—this is paid to him in a lump sum with interest, and strangely tax-free. If a player started in big-time soccer at twenty-one, and played fifteen years, averaging $100 per week, he would receive about $9,000—respectable, but not overwhelming. In fact, however, few men play fifteen years at the top.

Benefit games are given after five years of service, but only to star players, and only with the Football Association's approval. For a famous star one of these could bring in as much as £10,000, or at the current rate about $25,000.

But American players do not want to depend on the beneficent whim of the management. They want their blessings spelled out in black and white.

That the British have long been cognizant of the disparity between the salary and pension systems on opposite sides of the Atlantic is shown by the trenchant observation of Danny Branchflower of playing and television fame:

"I am a professional footballer. I love the game. Any work I put into it I put in because I want to. There is the old saying, 'What you put in you should get back.' But you don't get it back. I've got a family to keep and I like to keep them as well as I can. But there is no future in football for that. I read about an American signing a baseball contract for £30,000 [about $75,000]. It would take Stanley Matthews thirty years to earn that. It's ridiculous to me."

That was spoken while Branchflower's name was still in the headlines as one of England's finest players, and before the financial floodgates had opened to him in the United States. In 1967 seven men in baseball were in the $100,000 class: Willie Mays, Mickey Mantle, Hank Aaron, Frank Robinson, Roberto Clemente, Don Drysdale, and Juan Marichal. When the Boston Red Sox signed Carl Yastrzemski for 1968 the contract, with fringe benefits, was reputed to be close to $250,000.

105

More than fifty baseball players get $50,000 or more a year. Wilt Chamberlain is said to have earned $200,000 for the 1966–67 season with the Philadelphia 76ers of the National Basketball Association, and his new contract called for a raise. Young college football players have been signed to contracts that, including insurance and future benefits, are in the $500,000 range as a complete package.

It was not until 1961 that the ceiling was lifted on wages for English soccer players. It was then £20 or scarcely $60 a week. There are some critics who argue that the level of play was better when there was a lid on salaries. At least everyone on a team was paid the same, thereby avoiding the jealousies that are created when stars get inflated wages.

Of course payment of big salaries is dependent on gate receipts, and side benefits such as television revenues, and American sports admission prices are notoriously higher than elsewhere. Ordinary major-league baseball is in the $2 and $3 class and for the World Series goes up to $6, $8, and $12; professional football and hockey are in the $5 to $8 range with basketball close behind. By contrast English soccer clubs charge four shillings (about sixty cents) for standing room, and 12/6, 15s and £1 for seats—$1.25, $1.80, and $2.40. Crowds in England vary, but 40,000 to 50,000 is average for a good first-division team and 10,000 to 20,000 for a second-division game. As is the case with American professional teams, English soccer clubs are private companies and shareholders do not benefit greatly. But whereas the administration in American professional sports pays itself substantial salaries, directors of English soccer clubs are allowed only expenses and in most cases it is a matter of personal pride and nothing else to be listed as a director. Frequently wealthy directors of lowly clubs will pitch in with cash to save a team from going broke.

Yet before the impact of American salaries hit home, the financial lure of soccer dazzled the British. Archie Ledbrooke and Edgar Turner, in *Soccer from the Press Box,* one of the liveliest books on the game, wrote in 1955:

"Professionals ... on the whole get a better deal and a far easier time from their employers than most workers. For instance, how would you like a job with these conditions:

"Income: £1,400 (about $3,400) (part of it tax-free) a year.

"Work for two hours a day.

"Be entertained practically every other week-end at your firm's expense.

"Spend a fortnight nearly every year on a tour abroad (again at the firm's or someone else's expense).

"Have about eleven weeks summer holiday.

"Rent a fully-furnished £1,500 (and better) house at 25 shillings a week [little more than $3—admittedly a dazzling prospect to an American].

"Receive various free meals and entertainment.

"Be presented every Christmas with a turkey.

"All those things, a top class player with a little luck can get *from soccer alone.*"

Even allowing for inflation, the difference between the purchasing power of the dollar and the pound, and the fact this was written in 1955, few American college men could be lured into professional sports at the prospect of $3,400 a year even with a turkey thrown in. And the authors go on to say:

"In all fairness, it should be stated that a man must not only be a top class player himself, but belong to a club capable of winning all the honours for an income like this to be earned. It includes his salary (limited then to about $60 per week), his bonuses, his benefits and everything it is possible to earn, including the nine percent tax free Provident Scheme."

The contrast between English soccer and baseball is sharp, not only in salaries but above all in future security. In baseball the players contribute nothing to the pension plan. The fund is built on All-Star game and World Series revenues, a portion of the television fee, and by outright contributions of the club

107

owners, who have guaranteed a total of $4,100,000 a year to the players' pension fund.

A man who played only five years in the major leagues and elected to receive the pension benefits at the age of fifty would get $250 per month. If he waited until sixty-five it would be $643, plus Social Security. A man with twenty years in the majors would receive $600 monthly at the age of fifty, or if he waited until he was sixty-five he would get the princely pension of $1,487 monthly. Or consider the case of a ten-year player, not uncommon in baseball. If he elected pension pay at fifty he would get $500 monthly, or $686 at fifty-five, or $933 at sixty. If he waited until he was sixty-five he would get $1,288. And on top of all this the *average* pay in the major leagues is $23,000 yearly.

In addition baseball has a health-care program, and provides $50,000 in life insurance for each player with ten years or more service while he is active, and $25,000 after he leaves baseball up to the time his pension starts. Managers, coaches, and trainers also share in the pension benefits. No wonder young college players with both advanced baseball skills and training in a lucrative profession must ponder their careers carefully, and in some cases attempt to combine baseball with their profession.

Baseball has set high standards internationally, too. Salaries of $25,000 a year are not uncommon in Japan, both for imported Americans and for native Japanese. In fact, baseball experts believe there are at least a dozen Japanese who could make the grade in the American big leagues but are not interested because it would mean a cut in pay. In Mexico and the Caribbean baseball salaries, while not up to the Japanese level, are alluring in pinched national economies.

Baseball led the way in American sports. In 1961, fourteen years after baseball's pension plan was started, the National Football League put one into effect. Now with the merger of the NFL and the American Football League, the pension plans of both branches of professional football are being brought together.

The NFL uses receipts from the championship games, the Miami Playoff Bowl, the Pro Bowl, the College All-Star Game, and picture card rights to nourish its pension plan. As in baseball, the player contributes nothing. The money is invested both in fixed-income securities and in common stocks. Assuming the normal growth of common stocks to be 2.5 percent a year, a five-year player would get $437 monthly at sixty-five and a ten-year player $821. There are also fringe benefits in life and health insurance, to say nothing of the sum of about $25,000 that went to each player of the Green Bay Packers in the 1966–67 season by virtue of winning both the league championship and the misnamed Super Bowl.

Hockey has come a long way, too. Once the members of the Stanley Cup championship team received gold watches. They bought their own chains. Now they get more than $5,000 each. Once there was no pension. Now it ranges from $125 monthly for a five-year player who retires at forty-five up to $411 for the same man at sixty-five; from $500 monthly for a twenty-year player who retires at forty-five up to $1,640 for the same man at sixty-five. Hockey goes even further than baseball and football in providing pension benefits. A man who has only had three years service at the top can look forward to $75 monthly at forty-five, $246 monthly at sixty-five.

Professional basketball players almost went on strike in early 1967 for the liberalization of their pension plan (which was then only about $200 monthly for a veteran), an indication of how seriously the modern athlete regards his future security.

The North American Soccer League is fully cognizant of the pressure for securing the old age of athletes, but until the time comes when the crowds are big enough to underwrite the cost they are powerless to act. When and if that time comes, the repercussions around the soccer world will be violent.

109

12

The fantastic pool betting system
based on soccer in England
and around the world

———◆———

The English are bettors. So are Americans, but in England betting is legal and widespread. Bookies are recognized by law and even accept bets on credit. The most amazing aspect of English betting is the soccer pools, a mushrooming industry that employs tens of thousands, took in $310,681,200 in wages for the 1966–67 season before devaluation and paid the government $79,982,000 in taxes.

It is of course possible to bet on a single soccer game, as is widely done surreptitiously in the United States with football, baseball, and basketball. It is also possible to place a fixed-odds bet. The bettor, or the bookie, selects a specific list of games, usually small, and odds are quoted in advance of the games as to what the payoff will be if the bettor is successful.

But far and away the most popular form of betting is in the pools, in which comparatively small bets are placed on a complicated variety of games and on which the payoff, against gigantic odds, can run as high as £400,000 tax-free, or about $1,000,000.

The British pool system flourishes because of a peculiarity of the game that soccer critics regard as a weakness—the propensity for a large number of games on any given day to wind up as ties, either scoreless or 1–1 or 2–2. Instead of betting on winners or on the margin of victory, known in North America as the point spread, the British bet on lists of games they believe will result in ties.

J. Jervis Bernard originated the idea in Birmingham in the 1930's and set up a small shop. He advertised that his clients could select a series of games, pay him a few pennies, and that after he had skimmed off ten percent of the total take to cover his expenses, he would distribute the balance equitably among the winners. This, of course, is the totalizer principle. He soon found that ten percent for himself was insufficient.

The Puritan element objected to the wide-scale gambling, and in 1933 Parliament appointed a Royal Commission to investigate betting in the realm. It recommended the outlawing of the soccer pools. The hue and cry was so great, however, that the pools were finally legalized. They grew steadily in scope and opulence until World War II forced a consolidation of all the big operators into a single Unity Pools, which disbanded with the end of hostilities. The expansion since then has been amazing. The operation of the pools is now Britain's seventh biggest industry, reaching by sound estimate into six out of every ten homes in the land, and contributing massively to post office revenues in stamps and money orders, in addition to the direct tax paid the government.

In a sense the pools resemble the "numbers racket" in the United States in that the payoff is frequent—daily for the numbers, once weekly for the pools—and the investment is small with an outside chance of large returns.

In American numbers betting, wagers as low as ten cents can be made, although fifty cents to one dollar are more common.

111

The bettor selects a number of three digits or less. The method of payoff varies from city to city but is commonly based on the first three digits of the total sales each day of the New York Stock Exchange. Furtive individuals in poorer neighborhoods collect the bets and dispense the winnings, which can range from a few dollars up to $1,000 and more. Organized criminal syndicates skim off a large portion of the day's betting total and of course nothing is paid in taxes.

But instead of being clandestine as are the numbers, the English soccer pools are respectable and aboveboard. They are patronized by grey-haired grandmothers who never see a soccer game as well as teen-agers, together with the great mass of soccer fans.

What follows is a theoretical account of a permutation bet of ten shillings ($1.20) on the possibility of a combination of three games out of five all ending in draws.

On a midweek night a family in a half-timbered cottage in Dorset gathers around the dining table and decides on the games they believe will wind up as ties. They are rosy-cheeked, respectable, and about as far removed from the stereotype patrons of the American numbers racket as is conceivable. There is probably considerable jesting and a few cups of tea and a discussion of how the vast pot of gold will be divided when it comes in. Quite possibly no one there has seen a soccer game in years.

On this particular occasion our British friends have placed an "X" against five different games and written on the coupon "permute 3 from 5 10 bets" and risked ten shillings on the outcome, or one shilling on each of the "10 bets." Mathematically five different things, such as the numbers one to five, may be combined in groups of three a total of ten times, such as 1–2–3, 1–2–4, 3–5–2, etc. The betting firm will figure out all the combinations, or permutations, saving our reckless gamblers the effort.

The coupon looks something like the one used in illegal American football betting. It is placed in a pale-blue envelope (the color varies) that bears a black star in the corner (the symbol also varies) and carried the next morning to the post office where a postal money order is purchased. There is a long line waiting to buy money orders even though the village is small. The order is placed in the envelope, which is then sealed and mailed. Postal clerks are careful to apply the cancelling stamp which shows the date and hour of posting. Obviously bets posted after the start of games on Saturday are automatically rejected by the betting firm.

The envelope with the bet may be addressed to a firm in London or Liverpool or even other cities, but what the postal clerks are guided by is the color of the envelope and the symbol on it. These show the particular substation of the enormous betting firm to which the envelope is to be delivered.

When it arrives at the substation, elaborate and intricate security measures go into effect immediately (not always in the sequence described and with latitude for special checks made by different betting firms).

The envelope is first slit open along the seam and then sent to a big punching machine which drills needles through both envelope and coupon, grouped in different numbers or symbols to show the exact time the bet was received—this in case of any argument over bets made after the results of the matches are known.

Next the envelope and money order go to a particular girl who handles all the bets of our Dorset friends as well as the bets of all their neighbors. Betting clients are not listed by names but only by addresses. This is to facilitate delivery of the coupons each week. The mimeographed list of names and addresses of all bettors in any given London street or country village are all kept together so that when the coupons for the following week's games are mailed out, the letters are in effect presorted and handed to the post office clearly marked as to the exact locality of destination. Hit-and-miss mailing by the betting firms would bog down the British postal service.

The girl in charge of our Dorset village has before her the mimeograph plates of all her clients with a card attached showing spaces for each week of the year. She marks off receipt of the bet, sends the mimeograph plate on its way to stamp the name and address on an envelope that will contain next week's list of matches, and records the sum of money wagered.

The coupon is now microfilmed as a guard against claims after the results are known. It then goes to another girl for the first check after the results of Saturday's matches are known. As soon as these are received they are printed on cards that exactly correspond to the betting coupons. It is thus a simple matter to match up the five games on which the Dorset hopefuls placed an "X" against the actual results. Losing games, that is, games that did not end in a draw, are marked in light-colored pen through which the original "X" shows clearly. If one or more of the permutation combinations show as winners, the coupon is passed along to a supervisor. If all are losers, the coupon goes to another clerk who makes her own check using a pen of a different color. If both agree the coupon has no winner, it is placed in the discard where it is held only long enough to make sure no claims will be made against it, and then thrown away.

If the coupon has a winner, a second check is made, and finally a third one. The total of all the bets on the winning combination is figured, the thirty percent government tax is deducted along with the operating cost and profit margin of the betting firm, and the remaining money is allocated to the delighted gamblers.

In the pools where vast sums of money can be won, usually on bets much more complicated than the one described here, persons holding winning combinations are urged to make their claims on Monday by telegram or registered letter. Some of the "claims" are the result of faulty memory and can quickly be eliminated by a check of the microfilm records. Payment will be made even if no claim is entered, but by calling for claims the betting firms facilitate payment.

The Wednesday national newspapers carry the results. There is joy for a few, disappointment for millions. Pool payments can run into the thousands of pounds although much more modest payments are the rule. Because the government's share is skimmed off the top, there is no income tax on any winnings.

There was one black Saturday in England a few years ago when almost every soccer match ran true to form with the result that thousands of Englishmen went to sleep Saturday night in the happy knowledge that they had picked the right combination. Visions of vast fortunes danced in their minds, but on Wednesday the long list of winners came out and under the totalizer system the prize was a scant $15.

Along with the totalizer pools there are still the fixed-odds betting firms, which announce in advance exactly what they will pay on successful combinations, just as do the American football betting cards. Some Saturdays these firms can run heavily in the red, only to make it up over the season.

Since 1955 payment must accompany the pool bets. Prior to that many of the football pools operated on credit just as British racehorse bookies do to this day. The use of credit opened the way for dishonest bettors to flood firm's with various coupon combinations under a variety of names, and pay, of course, only on those that won. Keeping of betting files by addresses rather than by names curbed this.

The betting firms must contend with possible dishonesty within their own ranks, and elaborate checks are employed to make certain no girl can alter a coupon to give a friend a winner, or drop one of her own selection—made after the results are in—into the assembly line. Any envelopes with bets received after the games have been played must go unopened first to the perforating machine that marks the exact time they were received.

In case of complaints, which are bound to be numerous in an operation like this, due not to dishonesty but rather to inaccurate home records or even faulty memory, a photostat of the original coupon is sent to the complainer.

In addition to the money skimmed off by the government in taxes, the pools enrich the English post office incalculably. For anyone who bets by mail there is the four-penny payment for a postal money order under £1, known as the poundage, or eight pence for those daring souls who bet more than one pound, plus the four-penny first-class postage, and the return postage from the pool promoters who send out their coupons each week.

The average bet is difficult to pinpoint. For old-age pensioners it probably is between one and two shillings a week, or less than fifty cents. Sturdier souls may risk ten shillings or so. In many offices there are syndicates of employees placing bets as high as £20 or £30 a week, the chance of winning being greatly enhanced by the greater variety of combinations, but the fruits of success being similarly diluted by the wide participation.

The promotional booklets put out by the big pools are as dignified as insurance brochures. The emphasis is on security and the happy life that £100,000 can bring. Some even "guarantee" that bettors will receive a substantial payoff if they can pick eight winners (tied games) from a list of matches in the "treble chance."

Unfortunately, making it big in the pools does not always mean happiness and contentment. Mrs. Vivian Nicholson, a 29-year-old moviehouse usherette, thought her ship had come sailing home when her husband, Keith, won £152,319 (about $425,000 at the time). Four years of fun and honeymoon followed in which they were reported to have spent £70,000, but it ended abruptly when Nicholson, a coal miner previously, died in an automobile accident. The fancy car, naturally, had been bought out of his winnings.

116

In Houston's Astrodome, Peter Knowles (No. 10) of the Los Angeles Wolves (Wolverhampton of England) heads the ball brilliantly in close play near the goal against the Houston Stars (Bangu of Brazil) in a United Soccer Association indoors game.

A scene from the National Professional Soccer League's 1967 championship game in Baltimore between the Baltimore Bays and the Oakland Clippers. During the furious action some of the players seem suspended in the air.

Ferenc Puskas, center, who fled Hungary after the 1956 revolution and led Real Madrid to numerous titles, was signed by the San Francisco Gales of the United Soccer Association for the 1968 season as player-coach. The Gales later merged with Vancouver to form the Vancouver Royals.

Portugal's famous Eusebio, in white jersey, forces his way past two Russian defenders in the 1966 World Cup in London. The shot was stopped by Lev Yashin, goalie for the Soviet team.

The Houston Stars (Bangu of Brazil), in dark uniforms, play the Los Angeles Wolves (Wolverhampton of England) in a 1967 United States Soccer Association game in Houston's Astrodome—the only place where soccer is played on a regulation-sized field under a rocf.

Danny Branchflower, the unabashedly frank Columbia Broadcasting System commentator for the 1967 soccer season in the United States. He was formerly captain of Tottenham Hotspur, which in 1960–61 scored an extremely rare double, winning England's First Division championship and the Football Association Cup Final.

Now there are cup finals in the United States, too. Commissioner
Dick Walsh, right, presents the United Soccer Association's 1967
championship trophy to Jack Kent Cooke. Cooke's Los Angeles
Wolves (the Wolverhampton Wanderers of England), wearing
Washington's color, defeated Aberdeen of Scotland 6–5 in two
overtimes before 17,824 in the Los Angeles Memorial Coliseum.

Alfredo di Stefano (in light uniform) of Real Madrid, one of soccer's immortals, heads the ball towards the goal.

In England the pools contribute to some degree to the security of soccer players, but in other European nations such as Sweden and Italy, the pools support amateur sports, and build stadiums and swimming pools. Pools financed the 1960 Olympic Games in Rome.

The great success of the British pool system and its various imitations around the world, compared to the lukewarm public reception of, say, the New York State Lottery, leads to interesting conclusions.

First, it would seem that the ordinary man likes to bet in small sums on something that pays off frequently, like the soccer pools or American football betting cards or the underworld's numbers racket.

Second, it would seem that anyone who bets, on soccer, horse racing, baseball, or football, likes to pit his vaunted perceptiveness and know-how against that of his fellow men, rather than buy an antiseptic ticket in the hope a certain number will be drawn out of an enormous fishbowl.

Third, it is apparent the success of the soccer pool system is based on gigantic volume made up of tiny returns. What a legal pool with the possibility of big, tax-free payoffs would become in the United States is something that defies the imagination. The legislatures of the states of New Hampshire and New York have already given legal sanctity to lotteries. As the search for new tax sources becomes more and more acute, the possibility of using a form of the soccer pools may come to be considered.

117

13

The international scope of soccer

———◆———

Soccer is the dominant world sport. There is no rival. By the latest Federation Internationale de Football Associations estimate, there are between sixteen and twenty million active soccer players in the world, of which about seventy percent are in Europe. The total yearly audience runs into the scores of millions.

The Soviet Union has 3,800,000 registered players and West Germany 2,300,000, but Holland is the focal point of soccer fanaticism. Holland has 577,690 registered players, one out of every twenty-one citizens, the highest saturation anywhere.

Worldwide soccer really began in 1904 when France, Holland, Belgium, Switzerland and Denmark banded together to form the forerunner of FIFA, the world governing body. The sport grew spectacularly after the close of World War I and literally exploded after World War II so that by the mid-1960's soccer people talked of one billion fans and 100,000,000 players, counting schoolboys and informal teams beyond FIFA's registered players, and 200,000 soccer clubs. Even the statistics on referees are staggering. There are more than 500,000 in Europe, with Russia boasting 180,000 and Holland a hefty 8,833.

Soviet Russia has embraced the English-born game with fervor. In fact it is in soccer that the Russians come the closest to admitting the existence of professional athletes. It is an open secret that Lev Yashin, the redoubtable six-foot, 38-year-old Russian goalie and others on the nineteen teams that compose the Class A top league in the Soviet Union live quite handsomely. In addition to the top league, there are 237 other organized teams in the land (the financial rewards to whose players are considerably below the Class A scale), plus countless thousands of school and factory teams. All of this leads up, in an elimination tournament strikingly parallel to that in England for the Football Association Cup, to a final for the "Cup of the Soviet Union." There is always a cup in soccer, even Soviet soccer.

Soccer, or "futbol" as it is known in the Soviet Union, draws vast crowds at cut-rate prices in Russia. In Moscow the three principal stadiums—Central Lenin, capacity 103,000; Dynamo, 54,000; and Locomotive, 40,000—are completely sold out for all important matches at a ticket price scale ranging from fifty-five cents for the poorest seats up to $1.35 for the best. To an outside observer it would seem soccer is the safety valve of the Russians, played in the street by countless little Soviet boys kicking at plastic balls, and argued about over vodka and tea by millions of their elders.

Soccer, however, is not without its problems in the Soviet Union. In the autumn of 1967 Valery Voronin, a member of the national Russian team and a star for the Torpedo eleven, publicly confessed a variety of unspecified sins and barely escaped with his athletic skin. He was dropped from the national team and disqualified as a player for Torpedo, but his disqualification was suspended provided he toed the mark from then on.

"For some time I forgot about self-control, violated dis-

119

cipline and tarnished the high honor of Soviet sportsmen," he wrote in a letter published in *Komsomolskaya Pravda*, the Young Communist League's newspaper. Preceding this, one of Voronin's teammates also wrote a letter to the newspaper, rebuking him for the error of his ways:

"You got away with it. Of course Voronin is Voronin. For a long time I could not understand what motivated your actions. Today I know exactly, only one thing: your awareness of complete immunity."

This letter, penned by Anzor Kavazashvili, hinted darkly of a runaway trip to the Black Sea, vodka bouts, and unexcused absences from games, one of which forced an injured player to enter the match against doctor's orders:

"Of course we might have lost this match even with you, as we have had defeats this season even with all our best players. But now I am talking not about lost games and goals scored or missed, but about you, our comrade, who strayed from the proper path."

Alcoholism figured in the 1965 disciplinary action of the Soviet Football Federation in barring eight players for life. These players even lost the designation "Master of Sports," an indignity that Voronin was spared.

There is also a lighter side to soccer in the Soviet, or at least a confused side. What happened to the Bacigalupo team of Italy could only occur in a super-bureaucracy, where someone in the course of intricate paper-shuffling made the wrong notation. Bacigalupo came to Moscow expecting to play a casual game against a pickup team. Instead it was dispatched to the uttermost reaches of central Asia, pitted against some of the Soviet's finest teams in stadiums packed with 20,000 and 30,000 spectators, and treated as if it were Italy's national team. Unfortunately Bacigalupo is in the seventh division of the Italian amateur soccer league and the players are mostly teenagers or men well past their prime.

Russian girls, however, atoned for the drubbings that Bacigalupo took on the soccer field by showering the players with invitations to dates.

"The boys were so busy during the night that athletically they were not at their best," said the Bacigalupo manager.

In an Uzbek village police were called to surround the Italians' hotel when girls laid seige to it; they carried one player back into the lobby after he had climbed out a window to seek out an Uzbek beauty.

It is in Italy that the game has been brought to the highest level of remuneration for the players and at the same time done more for amateur sport than in any other nation. First-class Italian players average around $20,000 a year in salary and the betting pools underwrite an extensive athletic program.

At the opposite end of the scale are Swedish soccer players, who until the start of the 1967 season were strictly amateur in status. The good ones signed professional contracts in other nations. The removal of the amateur classification did not bring huge rewards, however. The Swedish Football Association authorized payment of about $30 to a player for a victory as compared to $20 previously, and $15 for a tie instead of $10, but it also permitted two- and three-year contracts and legal side benefits. Strangely enough no large sums of money are involved in Swedish transfer fees, but there are cases of $20,000 being paid to the Association by a club that succeeds in signing a player from another team and wants to make him eligible to play in two months instead of after the compulsory one-year quarantine.

In Australia, soccer is still second in national interest to Rugby football but the sport is on the rise. The six first division games in Sydney each weekend draw a total of 18,000. Exhibition games with teams like Manchester United have drawn 50,000.

Australia had its troubles with FIFA ten years ago and was outlawed but came back into the fold after what amounted to a fine of $56,000. There were plenty of top European players who wanted to live and play in Australia, but Australia did not have the money to pay their transfer fees. The players came anyway and were given well-paid jobs. FIFA suspended the Australian Football Association. After rocking along a few years without the benefit of any visits by famous soccer clubs, Australia applied for readmission and was told the $56,000 assessed was for transfer fees. An interest-free loan from an oil company helped make the payment.

In war-beset Vietnam there is soccer, too, and with gaudy flourishes. On the concluding day of the 1967 Armed Forces Sports week, the South Vietnamese Airborne jumped from helicopters high above Cong Hoa Stadium in Saigon, plummeted down for a few seconds carrying colored smoke steamers, and then pulled their ripcords and landed on the playing field. Their opponents, the South Vietnamese Air Force team, followed more prosaically in two helicopters. The main attraction of the day was a game between a United States Air Force team and one made up of men from all the armed services of South Vietnam. The Vietnamese won 3–1.

Although still a distant second to baseball, soccer has gained a strong hold in Japan, whose wiry athletes, like others in the Orient, relish a sport where lack of size is no great handicap.

The most amazing of all Far Eastern soccer teams is the 1966 squad that represented North Korea in the World Cup competition. It survived to the final round of eight, to the great surprise of Europeans, and finished fifth in the tournament. The stamina, speed, and strategy of the players was on a par with the best teams of Europe.

Shiro Otani, soccer's foremost partisan in Japan and a long-time devotee of the game, has a story in *The Charm of Soccer* of a strange game he devised to bolster the morale of the native Kanaka on New Britain Island in the South Pacific where he was stationed with the Japanese Navy. Food was short, cloth for the native robes was disappearing, and the

American air raids by October of 1943 had become severe. The Kanaka sensed the defeat of Japan and were in low spirits.

"The poor Kanaka seemed only happy when they found a ball and kicked it high up into the sky," Otani reports. "A friend of mine in the Navy Civil Administration Office once saw them kicking a ball and came to me with a suggestion. He proposed we hold a soccer game for the Kanaka. He found soccer balls in the storeroom of the Navy but did not know how to mark a field and set up goals.

"Although I had been a soccer player myself for more than ten years ever since I was in primary school I remembered only vaguely that the width of the goal should be eight paces and the height eight feet. I was so happy to hear the word 'soccer' that I plunged enthusiastically into efforts to arrange a game for the Kanaka.

"I had six bamboos brought over first of all. Then I paced off the width of the goal and determined the height by jumping up and down several times. The goal without nets was completed finally when the bamboo poles were driven into the ground and the crossbar lashed in place.

"I was worried whether enough Kanaka would come for the game since they were very scared of air raids, but on the very soccer day I knew I was wrong. Hundreds of Kanaka came in long lines even walking all the way from villages six and eight miles from Rabaul. Each line was led by a village chief and men and women had on their very best flowing robes. The Kanaka can be foppish, but they all looked particularly nice and happy on the day of the soccer game. They were really dressed up, and carried handbags made of palm leaves in which they put combs and cigarettes. Their hair was decorated with red flowers.

"They loved running around and kicking the ball all day long, skillfully lifting their robes to maneuver. It seemed as if they had hungered for a soccer game for a long time. I don't know why, but fortunately there was not a single air raid that

123

day. I had never expected to see a soccer game played by the Kanaka in Rabaul. It impressed me with the world-wide influence of soccer. The Kanaka really knew how to play the game. I assumed they had been kicking a soccer ball ever since they were under German rule before World War I."

Even the fury of war is not sufficient to extinguish the joy men find in kicking a ball.

14

*Cups and caps; soccer's intricate
system of national and world
competition*

———◆———

Soccer football is a game of cups and caps. There are no pennants, no gonfalons, no bunting. The cups, usually large and ornate silver trophies (except for the World Cup, originally put up in 1930 by Jules Rimet, president of the Federation Internationale de Football Associations, which is solid gold and worth over $100,000), stand as the ultimate prize in every kind of soccer competition: county, collegiate, league, national, and international. The caps are awarded to players each time they are selected on a national team. They are small, schoolboy-type caps with short visors in a variety of colors and emblems. From these arise the description of a soccer star as an athlete who has won a high number of caps. When Scotland plays Wales or Ireland plays England it is an "international" match carrying the honor of a cap just as much as when Russia plays Italy.

The various national Football Associations organize a wide

variety of international matches, usually at the close of the regular league seasons but sometimes during them. It is comparatively easy to put together a national team in soccer, i.e., one chosen from among the best players of all the available teams within a nation, to engage in these international matches. Although soccer depends heavily on teamwork and cooperation, there is none of the intricate timing and elaborate play patterns of American football. Hence the welding together of a national soccer team can usually be accomplished in a comparatively short span of time.

There is another kind of international competition in which intact teams compete. In fact, it is possible for a soccer team to compete simultaneously in its own league race, in its national cup tournament, and in one of the half-dozen European or other international tournaments.

Since England is the mother of the sport, and since all nations including Soviet Russia pattern their soccer structure on the English, an outline of the English soccer competition shows how the scheme works.

Regular play in the four top divisions starts in the autumn and proceeds through the winter and into the spring to determine the league champions, and of course the cup winners, on the basis of two points awarded for each victory and one for each tie. Almost simultaneously play starts in the Football Association's Cup tournament, but here one loss and a team is out. Special Saturdays are set aside for the Cup play. First-division teams are exempted from the preliminary rounds, in which even amateur teams can compete if deemed sufficiently strong by the Football Association. In case of a tie there is a replay. After two rounds have narrowed the field, the big professional clubs move in, making up a total of sixty-four teams. The third, fourth, fifth, and sixth rounds cut this to four for the semifinals. These then determine the two finalists for the big show in Wembley Stadium.

The F.A. Cup Final is in May, always at Wembley, and

always before a capacity crowd of 100,000 that includes royalty. Ticket charges for the Final are ten shillings for standing room up to £3 for the best grandstand seats. The chances of an ordinary fan getting his hands on a ticket are about on a par with those of an ordinary baseball fan who hopes to see a World Series game. The Football Association itself handles the tickets, and the two finalist clubs get the biggest share, with smaller percentages going to other professional clubs right down the line to amateur groups, which might get a pair. The big teams usually allow each player a few tickets to do with as he pleases, and the finalists often run a drawing to distribute tickets among their supporters. In spite of this diffuse handling of tickets, or perhaps because of it, there is a big black market.

Typical of Cup Finals was that of 1967 when the Tottenham Hotspurs defeated Chelsea 2–1 in an all-London Final, the fifth Cup the Spurs have won. The gate receipts for the match exceeded $300,000 and standing-room tickets sold on the sly for as high as $30.

There is no fixed percentage award to Cup Final winners and losers as there is in the World Series or professional football's championships. Each club decides how to reward its players, and the average for a man on the winning team is around $1,500. There have even been cases of players on losing teams receiving nothing. Of course there is a television fee for each player—the staggering sum of £5 per man, or less than $15.

Thus at the end of the season there are champions in each of the four top divisions of professional soccer in England, and a Football Association Cup champion as well, and only rarely will one team win both honors.

The First Division champion now is eligible for the big money tournament: the European Cup of National Champions. The F.A. Cup winner is eligible for the European Cup of Cup Winners' championship.

In the European Cup the teams meet on an at-home and away basis with the winner determined by goal aggregate, in which goals scored away from home count twice as much as those scored at home. This, like the F.A. Cup tournament, is conducted on a knockout basis. When only two teams are left the final match is played on neutral ground and one game decides all.

The winner is considered the European champion. Meanwhile a similar tournament has been proceeding in South America. The winners meet to determine the soccer club championship of the world, but this time the scoring rules are shifted. A victory counts for two points and a draw for one, both at home and away.

In 1967 this particular soccer championship produced fireworks galore. Celtic of Glasgow won the Scottish First Division championship and then the European championship; Racing Club of Argentina won in South America. In the first game of their final series, Celtic won at home 1–0. Then Racing won in Buenos Aires 2–1. That left the two teams tied at two points each so they played a third time on a neutral field in Montevideo. The soccer world is still shaking from the effects of that match, won by Racing 1–0.

Rioting broke out in the stands between the Uruguayans, some 65,000 in all, who were pro-Scot or anyway anti-Argentinian, and 20,000 Racing Club supporters from Buenos Aires. After bottles and rocks had been thrown police used tear gas to restore order. But worst of all, in the eyes of soccer purists, were the fights on the field. At the end of the game each team had only eight players left on the field, and in fact four Celtics had been dismissed by Referee Rodolfo Osorio. The fourth, Bertie Auld, sent off with one minute left to play, refused to leave the game and Osorio, rather than risk further rioting, let him stay. Two Racing players were dismissed and a third was lost through injuries. The Celtic management slapped fines totaling $8,250 on the eleven players who started the game as a stern reminder that brawling and soccer do not go together.

The lone goal was scored by Juan Carlos Cardenas after ten

minutes of play in the second half and it brought each Racing player a bonus of 500,000 pesos, admittedly not as lush as it sounds but still $1,440. Cardenas' shot was a header that got by the Celtic goalie, John Fallon, who was substituting for Ronnie Simpson. Simpson was hit on the head with a bottle before the previous game in Buenos Aires and was carried to the dressing room, groggy and bleeding.

Scottish sportswriters raised angry voices over the Simpson incident. Said John Rafferty in *The Scotsman:* "It was the most disgraceful incident I have ever seen on any soccer field—and this was the world championship." Declared Alex Cameron in *The Scottish Daily Mail:* "President Ongania of Argentina was sitting a dozen rows from me when this vile act occurred. The scene which followed, with officials running about and shouting madly at each other, has never been equalled." Rafferty went on to say of the Buenos Aires game itself that "Racing showed no remorse and with cold cruelty set about giving Simpson company in his misery. Almost every Celtic player was hacked or kicked without compassion, and the Uruguayan referee tolerated it all. Apart from wonder at the toleration of the referee, it was astonishing that athletes could be so cruel in cold blood."

What happened in the final match in Montevideo was scarcely calculated to mollify the Scots. On that sad occasion Celtic players took it upon themselves to inflict punishment after repeated fouls—as they saw it—had gone unpunished. Sir Stanley Rous, the FIFA president, saw what happened at Montevideo and promptly announced that hereafter FIFA itself would appoint the referee and linesmen for such matches. He also advocated spread of the tournament to include participation from North America, Central America, Asia, Australia, and Africa, hopefully on a somewhat more gentlemanly basis.

In the other big European tournament, the Cup of Cup Winners' championship, the European Federation is the organizer and play is somewhat more orderly. Winners of national cups qualify, and the tournament, also with knockout rules, is decided on a home and away basis, with the final on neutral grounds, but there is no South American aftermath.

Europe also boasts an Inter-Cities Fairs Cup, originally restricted to European cities which had held trade fairs, but now conducted on an invitational basis. Still another soccer tournament is the Nations Cup. National teams qualify for this after playing matches against other teams in their group. The winner of the British championship, which involves England, Northern Ireland, Scotland, and Wales, enters this competition.

The World Cup is the greatest and gaudiest of all soccer championships. It was the brainchild of Jules Rimet, who was elected president of the Federation Internationale de Football Associations in 1920 and remained at its head until 1954. In fact, the true name of the golden cup trophy is the Jules Rimet Trophy. He advocated worldwide competition with great persuasiveness and felt that professional soccer should have a championship akin to the amateur crown provided by the Olympic Games. Olympiads have been staged every four years from 1896 on except when war interfered, and Rimet proposed a similar four-year span for the World Cup scheduled to fall between the Games. Thus the 1964 Olympics took place in Toyko and the 1966 World Cup in London, with the 1968 Games set for Mexico City, and, coincidentally, the 1970 World Cup for the same place.

It was the soccer tournament of the 1924 Olympic Games in Paris that finally pushed professional soccer into its own tournament. For the first time this brought soccer competition between Europe and the Americas. Both the United States and Uruguay were entered. The Europeans looked down their noses at the alien invaders, but Uruguay, playing with finesse and poise, swept aside all opposition and in the end defeated Switzerland 3–0 before a crowd of 50,000 in Colombes Stadium. The team achieved instant popularity, and Henri Delauney, the secretary of the French Football Association, was able to

130

declare to the 1926 FIFA Congress: "Today international football can no longer be held within the confines of the Olympics; and many countries where professionalism is now recognized and organized can not any longer be represented there by their best players."

The first World Cup was held in Uruguay in 1930. Uruguay offered to pay all expenses, including travel, of the competing teams as well as erect in the brief span of eight months a stadium in the heart of Montevideo capable of holding close to 100,000. European nations suddenly developed cold feet. England was out the picture anyway, as it was not a member of FIFA; King Carol of Romania, an ardent soccer fan, had to intervene in order to send a team, and he selected it himself; then Belgium and Yugoslavia came in reluctantly; and finally France, out of a sense of obligation to FIFA, accepted. These four nations represented Europe.

The pattern of World Cup play was established from the outset. The contesting teams were divided into four pools and after round-robin play the winners in each pool advanced to the semifinals. In the 1930 final, Uruguay defeated Argentina 4–2. Now the prestige of the World Cup is so great that one hundred nations vie in an elaborate series of preliminaries for the honor of a place in the sixteen-team finals.

Soccer promoters around the world seem to be as adept as their American counterparts in baseball, basketball, football, and hockey in devising elaborate play-offs leading to a variety of championship titles with the ultimate effect of bolstering sporting exchequers. The Americans get the points on generosity, since their players fare better financially than do soccer players in international championship tournaments.

15

The future of soccer in the United
States and Canada

———◆———

What is the future of soccer in the United States and Canada? The experiment now under way is unlike anything ever tried before in any sport. New professional leagues have been started from scratch in recent years in football and basketball and have waxed prosperous. These sports, however, are solidly rooted. Soccer, although it has a devoted following in North America and much wider participation than is generally realized both on the sandlot and club level and in prep schools and colleges, nevertheless has hitherto not been national in appeal.

If there is any parallel—and this must give great encouragement to the professional promoters—it can be found in hockey, a sport that greatly resembles soccer in speed and format. Hockey, in spite of college-level enthusiasm, has less support at the grass-roots level in the United States than has soccer, and yet it has been phenomenally successful. Americans may not play it much, but they love to watch it. Its strong hold on colder Canada where every schoolchild plays it on frozen ponds

132

is more readily understandable. The National Hockey League, which doubled in size at the start of the 1967 season, generally plays to packed houses, and only two of its twelve teams are located in Canada. Furthermore, the United States has embraced hockey enthusiastically in spite of the fact that virtually all players come from Canada. This defies the theory that for a sport to be successful it must have a large proportion of native-born players. If Americans like hockey in the winter there seems no sensible reason why they should not take to soccer in the summer.

Professional soccer in the United States and Canada has many plus signs in its ledger.

The new venture is well financed and well managed, two vital factors in launching any kind of sports promotion.

The merger of the National Professional Soccer League and the United Soccer Association to form the North American Soccer League has eliminated costly rival teams in a half-dozen cities. It has also brought worldwide recognition to all the professional teams involved instead of only half of them. By dividing the new league into an eastern and western division travel expenses will be materially reduced and natural rivalries encouraged.

The national television contract with the Columbia Broadcasting System is of inestimable value in recruiting fans for the game. People tend to want to see in the flesh anything they have watched at any length on a television screen. The audience ratings for soccer games in 1967 were surprisingly high, further proof of the appeal of the game.

The program that all of the professional clubs have undertaken in sending players and coaches to talk at school clinics and soccer practice sessions is building fan support at the adolescent level, a most important one.

And finally, only in soccer can the average or even small-sized schoolboy see the hope of stardom that is inexorably denied him in football, basketball, and hockey, and to a considerable extent in baseball.

Before the 1967 season ended there was growing evidence of strong local identification with teams, particularly in Baltimore, Atlanta, Houston, Oakland and Los Angeles, a "must" factor in the success of any professional sport.

Whether all these promising points actually bring soccer to a well-deserved success in North American sport depends upon some important ifs:

If fan support continues to grow to the point where at least most of the clubs are breaking even in expenses before 1970; *if* television can be adroitly manipulated to promote larger soccer audiences as was done so skillfully in professional football; *if* the power structure of soccer, the United States Soccer Football Association and its Canadian counterpart, can be made into an efficient, disciplined organization like the English Football Association; *if* personalities of the game begin to emerge on North American soil; and *if* the promoters do not too easily lose heart that the day is coming when the United States and Canada will join the rest of the world in a game that is without equal for speed, finesse, excitement and drama.

GLOSSARY

———◆———

Angle of Possibility—An imaginary angle made by projecting a line from a player about to shoot a goal to each side of the goalposts; the wider the angle the better the chance of scoring.

Backup—A defensive player drops behind another defensive player to support him.

Ball—Ever since 1889 the soccer ball has been standardized as being not less than 27 inches nor more than 28 inches in circumference, and in international matches the weight must be between twelve and fifteen ounces at the start of the game. It is made of leather and is inflated.

Blocking—It is legal in soccer to obstruct (block) the forward movement of an opponent by moving slowly forward in front of him; if the blocker does not back into his opponent and continues to move away from him the obstruction is aboveboard.

Center Forward—Soccer's score maker, the possessor of a powerful kick and the ability to head the ball into the nets with deadly accuracy; often a taller, stronger man than the others on the field.

Center Halfback—In the classic lineup at the start of the game this man plays some ten paces back of the center forward; as a halfback he is part of both the offense and the defense, and as the center half he can roam more than the other two halfbacks.

Center Kick—A kick from near the sidelines, or more properly, the touchlines, to the center of the field in front of the goal, meant to put the ball in position for a score.

Charging—A legal, sometimes violent attack on an opponent

who has possession of the ball, the object being to get control of the ball. The arms and hands must be held close to the body and only the shoulder may be used in making contact; one foot must always remain on the ground.

Chest Trapping—Stopping a kicked ball with the chest, arms held back, and leaning backwards to induce it to trickle to the ground in such a manner that it can quickly be controlled.

Clearing Kick—Any kick that sends a ball out of danger from one end of the field towards the other.

Combination—A play involving two or more players on a team with the object of outmaneuvering the opponents.

Corner Kick—A direct free kick made from the one-yard, pie-shaped portion of a circle in the corner of the field and capable of scoring a goal if the kicker can manage a hard curve; it is awarded to the attacking team when a member of the defending team is the last to touch the ball before it goes over the goal line but not into the nets.

Cross—Any kick from one side of the field to the other.

Direct Free Kick—A penalty kick which can score a goal directly, in most cases the result of a personal foul; if awarded within the penalty area only the goalie is between the kicker and the nets, if outside the penalty area defending players can lock arms to present a protective wall in front of the goal but ten yards from the kicker.

Diving—The act of the goalie in throwing himself at a ball to deflect it from the nets and prevent a score.

Dribbling—Controlling the ball with the feet while running downfield; not to be confused with bouncing the ball as in basketball.

Flick Pass—Usually made while dribbling, this is a short and deceptive kick of the ball to one side to a teammate.

Forward—A member of the attack, either as left or right wing, center forward, or inside left or right; the five men on a soccer team most apt to be down the field near the opponent's goal.

136

Fouling—An illegal use of the hands or the body, chiefly on defense, which can lead to a direct free kick for the opposite team.

Fullback—There are two of these, left and right, usually stationed on either side of the goalie. As in American football, fullbacks in soccer tend to be bigger and stronger than the other players, but unlike their counterparts in football they are purely members of the defense.

Goalie—The man stationed directly in front of the nets and charged with the responsibility of preventing a score; he is the only player privileged to use his hands on the ball or to advance it within the penalty box by bouncing it on the ground between steps.

Goal Area—The goal area is inside the penalty area; it is directly in front of the nets and measures twenty yards by six yards. The ball is placed anywhere in the goal area when a goal kick is being taken; in the goal area, if the goalkeeper has possession of the ball or is obstructing an opponent he can be charged.

Goal Kick—A kick taken by a defending team from the goal area after the ball crosses the goal line—but not into the nets—having been last touched by an attacking player.

Halfback—There are two of these, left and right, stationed on either side of the center half at the start of the game and like him used both on offense and defense.

Half Volley Kick—A ball kicked simultaneously as it hits the ground.

Heading—The art of using the head, usually the flat, center part of the forehead, to propel a ball intercepted in midair in any direction, but most frequently utilized in an effort to score a goal.

Head-On Tackle—A defensive action done with the shoulder, arms at side, aimed at taking the ball away from an opponent who is dribbling it downfield.

137

Heeling—A backward pass of the ball made with the heel of the foot, usually while dribbling.

Indirect Free Kick—A kick awarded for a technical violation of the rules from which a goal cannot be scored directly.

Interception—Any legal action by the defending team that intercepts a pass of the attackers.

Linesmen—The two officials that patrol either side of the field and decide who gets possession of the ball when it goes out of bounds; used by the referee as consultants when he is not in a position to decide for himself.

Mark—The defensive action of shadowing a man.

Nets—The netting strung around the goalposts.

Obstructing—The same as blocking.

Off Side—An offensive player is off side unless there are two opposing players, one of whom may be the goalie, between him and his opponent's goal, unless he or his opponent last touched the ball or is in his own half of the field.

Pass—Transfer of the ball from one player to a teammate; in soccer a pass is made by kicking the ball instead of throwing it as in basketball or football.

Penalty Area—The zone, 44 yards by 18 yards, in front of the goal in which the goalie is permitted to use his hands on the ball and in which a personal foul by a defending player brings a direct penalty kick from a marked spot twelve yards from the goal with no one between the kicker and nets except the goalkeeper.

Penalty Kick—See Penalty Area; if the offense is committed outside the penalty area but close enough to threaten a score the defending players can line up with locked arms ten yards from the kicker in an effort to avert a goal.

Pitch—British name for the playing field.

Referee—The only official on the playing field; the man in complete and unquestioned control of the game.

Save—The prevention of a goal by the goalkeeper.

Side—A team. This use of the word, strange as it may sound to American ears, restores it to its original sense, as in the question, "Whose side are you on anyway?"

Tackle—To gain possession of the ball by hooking it away from a dribbler with the feet.

Throw-in—When the ball goes across the sideline, or touchline, it is put back in play by the opponents of the team that touched it last before it went out. The throw back into play must be made over the head, with both hands on the ball and both feet on the ground and off the field of play.

Trap—To get possession of a ball in the air by use of the head, chest, arms, legs or feet—but never the hands.

Touchline—The boundary at each side of the field.

Wing—One of the two forward players stationed at each side of the field; in classic soccer a small, fast man adept at getting possession of the ball and feeding it, by a cross (kick) to the center forward, who then attempts to score.

139

APPENDIX

WORLD CUP WINNERS

1930 in Uruguay

Champions: Uruguay
Second: Argentina
Third: United States
Fourth: Yugoslavia

1934 in Italy

Champions: Italy
Second: Czechoslovakia
Third: Germany
Fourth: Austria

1938 in France

Champions: Italy
Second: Hungary
Third: Brazil
Fourth: Sweden

1942 and 1946 canceled by World War II
1950 in Brazil

Champions: Uruguay
Second: Brazil
Third: Sweden
Fourth: Spain

1954 in Switzerland

Champions: West Germany
Second: Hungary
Third: Austria
Fourth: Uruguay

1958 in Sweden

Champions: Brazil
Second: Sweden
Third: France
Fourth: West Germany

1962 in Chile

Champions: Brazil
Second: Czechoslovakia
Third: Chile
Fourth: Yugoslavia

1966 in England

Champions: England
Second: West Germany
Third: Chile
Fourth: Russia

UNITED STATES NATIONAL CHALLENGE CUP

The United States National Challenge Cup, originated in 1914, is similar in concept to the English Football Association competition which climaxes in the Cup Final in Wembley. The National Challenge Cup is a solid silver trophy and the competition is open both to professional and amateur soccer teams. Eliminations cut the field to two finalists.

YEAR	CHAMPIONS		RUNNERS-UP	
1914	Brooklyn Field Club	2	Brooklyn Celtic	1
1915	Bethlehem Steel	3	Brooklyn Celtic	1
1916	Bethlehem Steel	1	Fall River Rovers	0
1917	Fall River Rovers	1	Bethlehem Steel	0
1918	Bethlehem Steel	2	Fall River Rovers	2
	Bethlehem Steel	3	Fall River Rovers	0
1919	Bethlehem Steel	2	Paterson	0
1920	Ben Millers	2	Fore River	1
1921	Robbins Dry Dock	4	Scullin Steel	2
1922	Scullin Steel	3	Todd Shipyard	2
1923	Paterson	2	Scullin Steel	2
	(Awarded to Paterson by default)			
1924	Fall River	4	Vesper Buick	2
1925	Shawsheen	3	Canadian Club	0
1926	Bethlehem Steel	7	Ben Millers	2
1927	Fall River	7	Holly Carburetor	0
1928	New York Nationals	2	Bricklayers	2
	New York Nationals	3	Bricklayers	0
1929	Hakoah All-Stars	2	Madison Kennels	0
	Hakoah All-Stars	3	Madison Kennels	0
	(First year of deciding championship by two out of three-game series)			
1930	Fall River	7	Bruell Insurance	2
	Fall River	2	Bruell Insurance	1

YEAR	CHAMPIONS		RUNNERS-UP	
1931	Fall River	6	Bricklayers	2
	Fall River	1	Bricklayers	1
1932	New Bedford	3	Stix, Baer, and Fuller	3
	New Bedford	5	Stix, Baer, and Fuller	2
1933	Stix, Baer, and Fuller	1	New York Americans	0
	Stix, Baer, and Fuller	2	New York Americans	1
1934	Stix, Baer, and Fuller	4	Pawtucket Rangers	2
	Stix, Baer, and Fuller	2	Pawtucket Rangers	3
	Stix, Baer, and Fuller	5	Pawtucket Rangers	0
1935	Central Breweries	5	Pawtucket Rangers	2
	Central Breweries	1	Pawtucket Rangers	1
	Central Breweries	1	Pawtucket Rangers	3
	(Central Breweries awarded championship on total goals)			
1936	Philadelphia Americans	2	St. Louis Shamrocks	2
	Philadelphia Americans	3	St. Louis Shamrocks	1
1937	New York Americans	0	St. Louis Shamrocks	1
	New York Americans	4	St. Louis Shamrocks	2
	(New York Americans awarded championship on total goals)			
1938	Sparta	4	St. Mary's Celtic	0
	Sparta	4	St. Mary's Celtic	2
1939	St. Mary's Celtic	1	Manhattan Beer	0
	St. Mary's Celtic	4	Manhattan Beer	1
1940	Baltimore Soccer Club	0	Sparta	0
	Baltimore Soccer Club	2	Sparta	2
	(No deciding game played due to defense emergency difficulties)			
1941	Pawtucket	4	Chrysler	2
	Pawtucket	4	Chrysler	3
1942	Gallatin	2	Pawtucket	1
	Gallatin	4	Pawtucket	2
1943	Brooklyn Hispano	2	Morgan Strasser	2
	Brooklyn Hispano	4	Morgan Strasser	2
1944	Brooklyn Hispano	4	Morgan Strasser	0
	(Single game due to war restrictions)			
1945	Brookhattan	4	Cleveland Americans	1
	Brookhattan	2	Cleveland Americans	1
1946	Chicago Vikings	1	Ponta Delgada	1
	Chicago Vikings	2	Ponta Delgada	1

YEAR	CHAMPIONS		RUNNERS-UP	
1947	Ponta Delgada	6	Sparta	1
	Ponta Delgada	3	Sparta	2
1948	Simpkins	3	Brookhattan	2
	(Single game)			
1949	Morgan	0	Philadelphia Nats	1
	Morgan	4	Philadelphia Nats	2
	(Morgan awarded championship on total goals)			
1950	Simpkins	2	Ponta Delgada	0
	Simpkins	1	Ponta Delgada	1
1951	German Hungarian	2	Heidelberg	4
	German Hungarian	6	Heidelberg	2
	(German Hungarian awarded championship on total goals)			
1952	Harmarville	3	Philadelphia Nats	4
	Harmarville	4	Philadelphia Nats	1
	(Harmarville awarded championship on total goals)			
1953	Falcons of Illinois	2	Harmarville	0
	Falcons of Illinois	1	Harmarville	0
1954	New York Americans	1	Kutis	1
	New York Americans	2	Kutis	0
1955	Eintracht	2	Danish Americans	0
	(Single game)			
1956	Harmarville	0	Chicago Schwaben	1
	Harmarville	3	Chicago Schwaben	1
1957	Kutis	3	Hakoah New York	0
	Kutis	3	Hakoah New York	1
1958	Los Angeles Kickers	2	Pompei Baltimore	1
	(Single game)			
1959	San Pedro Canvasbacks	4	Fall River	3
	(Single game)			
1960	Philadelphia Ukrainian	5	Los Angeles Kickers	3
	(Single game)			
1961	Philadelphia Ukrainian	2	Los Angeles Scots	2
	Philadelphia Ukrainian	5	Los Angeles Scots	2
1962	New York Hungarian	3	San Francisco Scots	0
	(Single game)			
1963	Philadelphia Ukrainian	1	Los Angeles Armenian	0
	(Single game)			

YEAR	CHAMPIONS		RUNNERS-UP	
1964	Los Angeles Kickers	2	Philadelphia Ukrainian	2
	Los Angeles Kickers	2	Philadelphia Ukrainian	0
1965	New York Ukrainian	1	Hansa Chicago	1
	New York Ukrainian	3	Hansa Chicago	0
1966	Philadelphia Ukrainian	1	Orange County, Calif.	0
	Philadelphia Ukrainian	3	Orange County, Calif.	0
1967	Greek-American, New York	4	Orange County, Calif.	2

(Single game)

UNITED STATES NATIONAL AMATEUR CUP

YEAR	CHAMPIONS		RUNNERS-UP	
1924	Fleisher Yarn	3	Swedish-American	0
1925	Toledo	3	McLeod Council	1
1926	Defenders	1	Heidelberg	0
1927	Heidelberg	3	LaFlamme Cobblers	0
1928	(No game, unable to obtain suitable grounds)			
1929	Heidelberg	9	First German Soccer Club	0
1930	Raffies	3	Gallatin	3

(Championship awarded to Raffies when Gallatin was unable to complete arrangements for a replay)

YEAR	CHAMPIONS		RUNNERS-UP	
1931	Goodyear	1	Black Cats	1
	Goodyear	2	Black Cats	0
1932	Cleveland Shamrock	2	Santa Christo	1
1933	German-American	5	McKnight Beverage	1
1934	German-American	2	Heidelberg	1
1935	W. W. Riehl	3	All-American Cafe	0
1936	Brooklyn Soccer Club	2	Castle Shannon	1
1937	Trenton Highlander	1	Castle Shannon	0
1938	Ponta Delgada	2	Heidelberg	0
1939	St. Michael's	3	Gallatin	1
1940	Morgan Strasser	1	Firestone	0
1941	Fall River	2	Chrysler	1
1942	Fall River	4	Morgan Strasser	3
1943	Morgan Strasser	4	Santa Maria	1
1944	Eintracht	5	Morgan Strasser	2
1945	Eintracht	1	Rafterys	0
1946	Ponta Delgada	5	Castle Shannon	2
1947	Ponta Delgada	4	Curry Veterans	1
1948	Ponta Delgada	4	Curry Veterans	1
1949	Elizabeth	6	Zenthoefer	1
1950	Ponta Delgada	0	Harmarville	0
	Ponta Delgada	4	Harmarville	1

YEAR	CHAMPIONS		RUNNERS-UP	
1951	German Hungarian	4	Harmarville	3
1952	Raiders	3	Lusitano	1
1953	Ponta Delgada	2	Chicago Slovaks	0
1954	Beadling	2	Simpkins	5
	Beadling	5	Simpkins	1
1955	Heidelberg Tornadoes	2	Chicago Eagles	2
	Heidelberg Tornadoes	5	Chicago Eagles	0
1956	Kutis	1	Philadelphia Ukrainian	0
1957	Kutis	1	Rochester Ukrainian	0
1958	Kutis	2	Beadling	1
1959	Kutis	5	St. Andrew Scots	0
	Kutis	2	St. Andrew Scots	2
1960	Kutis	4	Patchogue, New York	0
1961	Kutis	11	Italian-Americans	0
	Kutis	3	Italian-Americans	3
1962	Carpathia Kickers	4	American Hungarian	0
1963	Italian-Americans	1	St. Ambrose	0
1964	Schwaben	4	German Hungarian	0
1965	German Hungarian	6	St. Ambrose	0
1966	Chicago Kickers	5	Italian-Americans	2
1967	Italian-Americans	2	Kutis	0

CANADIAN NATIONAL CHAMPIONS

1913   Norwood Wanderers
1914   Norwood Wanderers
1915   Winnipeg Scots
1916   No competition, war.
1917   No competition, war.
1918   No competition, war.
1919   Grand Tunk, Quebec
1920   Westinghouse, Ontario
1921   Toronto Scots
1922   Calgary Hillhurst
1923   Nanaimo, British Columbia
1924   United Western, Winnipeg
1925   Ulster United, Toronto
1926   United Western, Winnipeg
1927   Nanaimo, British Columbia
1928   New Westminster Royals
1929   Canadian National Railways, Montreal
1930   New Westminster Royals
1931   New Westminster Royals
1932   Toronto Scots
1933   Toronto Scots
1934   Verdun, Montreal
1935   Aldreds
1936   New Westminster Royals
1937   Johnston Nationals
1938   North Shore, Vancouver
1939   Radicals, Vancouver
1940   No competition, war.
1941   No competition, war.
1942   No competition, war.
1943   No competition, war.

1944 No competition, war.
1945 No competition, war.
1946 Ulster United, Toronto
1947 St. Andrew's, Vancouver
1948 Carsteel, Montreal
1949 North Shore, Vancouver
1950 Vancouver City
1951 Ulster United, Toronto
1952 Steelco Montreal
1953 New Westminster Royals
1954 A.N. and A.F. Scottish Winnipeg
1955 New Westminster Royals
1956 Haleces, Vancouver
1957 Ukrainia, Montreal
1958 New Westminster Royals
1959 Alouettes
1960 New Westminster Royals
1961 Concordia, Montreal
1962 Winnipeg Scots
1963 No competition.
1964 Columbus, Vancouver
1965 Firefighters, Vancouver
1966 New Westminster Royals
1967 Vally Mena United, Toronto

OLYMPIC GAMES SOCCER CHAMPIONS

1900—Great Britain
1904—Canada
1906—Denmark
1908—Great Britain
1912—Great Britain
1916—No competition, war.
1920—Belgium
1924—Uruguay
1928—Uruguay
1932—No competition, depression.
1936—Italy
1940 and 1944—No competition, war.
1948—Sweden
1952—Hungary
1956—Russia
1960—Yugoslavia
1964—Hungary

UNITED SOCCER ASSOCIATION

1967 Final Standings

EASTERN DIVISION

	W	L	T	PTS.	GF	GA *
Washington Whips (Aberdeen, Scotland)	5	2	5	15	19	11
Cleveland Stokers (Stoke City, England)	5	3	4	14	19	13
Toronto City (Hibernian, Scotland)	4	3	5	13	23	17
Detroit Cougars (Glentoran, Northern Ireland)	3	3	6	12	11	18
New York Skyliners (Cerro, Uruguay)	2	4	6	10	15	17
Boston Shamrock Rovers (Shamrock Rovers, Ireland)	2	7	3	7	12	26

WESTERN DIVISION

	W	L	T	PTS.	GF	GA
Los Angeles Wolves (Wolverhampton, England)	5	2	5	15	21	14
San Francisco Gales (A.D.O., Netherlands)	5	4	3	13	25	19
Chicago Mustangs (Cagliari, Italy)	3	2	7	13	20	14
Houston Stars (Bangu, Brazil)	4	4	4	12	19	18
Vancouver Royal Canadians (Sunderland, England)	3	4	5	11	20	28
Dallas Tornadoes (Dundee, Scotland)	3	6	3	9	14	23

(The United Soccer Association followed the traditional worldwide system and awarded two points for a victory and one for a tie.)

* Won, Lost, Ties, Points, Goals For, Goals Against

152

Championship Play-off

July 15, 1967, Los Angeles (two overtimes)

| Los Angeles Wolves | 1 | 3 | 1 | 1–6 |
| Washington Whips | 1 | 3 | 1 | 0–5 |

Los Angeles scoring: Dave Burnside 3, Peter Knowles, Derek Dougan, Bobby Thomson
Washington scoring: Francis Munro 3, Jim Smith, Jim Storrie
Attendance: 17,824

NATIONAL PROFESSIONAL SOCCER LEAGUE

1967 Final Standings

	W	L	T	PTS.	GF	GA
Baltimore Bays	14	9	9	162	53	47
Philadelphia Spartans	14	9	9	157	53	43
New York Generals	11	13	8	143	60	58
Atlanta Chiefs	10	12	9	135	51	46
Pittsburgh Phantoms	10	14	7	132	59	74

WESTERN DIVISION

Oakland Clippers	19	8	5	185	64	34
St. Louis Stars	14	11	7	156	54	57
Chicago Spurs	10	11	11	142	50	55
Toronto Falcons	10	17	5	127	59	70
Los Angeles Toros	7	15	10	113	42	61

(The National Professional Soccer League awarded six points for a victory and three for a tie with every goal up to and including three scored by either team also counting for one point.)

Championship Play-offs

September 3, 1967, at Baltimore

Baltimore Bays	0	1–1
Oakland Clippers	0	0–0

Baltimore scoring: Dennis Viollet
Attendance: 16,619

September 9, 1967, at Oakland

Oakland Clippers	3	1–4
Baltimore Bays	1	0–1

Oakland scoring: Dragan Djukic 3, Edgat Marin
Baltimore scoring: Guy St. Vil
Attendance: 9,037

(Oakland won championship on basis of total goals in both games.)

THE NATIONAL COLLEGIATE ATHLETIC
ASSOCIATION'S SOCCER TOURNAMENT

YEAR	CHAMPIONS		RUNNERS-UP	
1959	St. Louis	5	Bridgeport	2
1960	St. Louis	3	Maryland	2
1961	Westchester	2	St. Louis	0
1962	St. Louis	4	Maryland	3
1963	St. Louis	3	Navy	0
1964	Navy	1	Michigan State	0
1965	St. Louis	1	Michigan State	0
1966	San Francisco	5	Long Island University	2
1967	Michigan State and St. Louis declared co-champions when their scoreless game was terminated because of bad weather.			

Index